CHAPTER : 1
CONCEPT OF COMPUTER

Structure

1.0 Objective

1.1Introduction

1.2 Usage of Computer
1.3 Anatomy of a Digital Computer

1.0 Objective

Objective of this lesson get acquaint the reader to the basic units of a computer system; learn about the digit symbols, base, and representation of various number systems, methods of number system conversions; understand with the coding schemes for the internal storage of characters.

1.1 Introduction

Computer is an electronic device, which accepts data, processes it and outputs the results in the form of reports. Original objective of computer was to make fast calculations, but the modern computers besides performing fast calculations can store large volume of data, process and retrieve data as and when desired. Hence computers are also known as data processors.

Computer is a system. A system is a group of integrated parts to achieve a common objective. Computer is made up of integrated parts (input, control, ALU, storage and output unit) .All the parts work together to process data.

The computer accepts input and outputs data in an alphanumeric form. Internally it converts the input data to meaning binary digits, performs the instructed operations on the binary data, and transforms the data from binary digit form to understandable alphanumeric form.

1.2 Usage of Computers in Everyday life

Computers have a significant impact on everyday life in nearly all areas.

Computers are used in:

¾ Airline and Railway Reservations

¾ Medical Diagnosis

¾ Whether Forecasting

¾ Payment of telephone and electricity bills

¾ Banking

¾ Space research

¾ Online Education

¾ Sending and receiving data throughout the world using internet

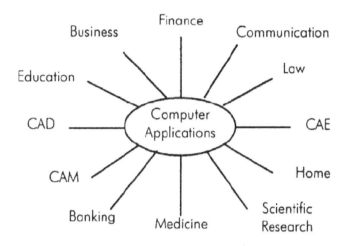

Figure 1.1 Usage of Computer

1.3 Anatomy of a Digital Computer (MODEL OF A DIGITAL COMPUTER)

There are three major components of a digital computer:

(i)   Input Unit

(ii)   Central Processing Unit
> (a) Memory
> (b) ALU (Arithmetic & Logic Unit)
> (c) Control Unit

(iii)   Output Unit

General arrangement of various units is shown in Figure 1.2

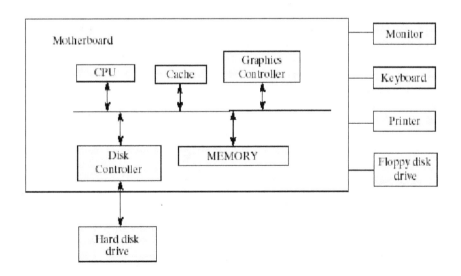

INPUT UNIT

This unit contains devices with the help of which we enter data into computer. This unit is linked between user and computer. Input devices translate the human-being information into the form understandable by a computer.

The input, output and storage devices are described as on line, when they are directly connected to the CPU, when not connected directly they are described as off-line.

Examples of input devices:
{i) Keyboard (ii) VDU (Visual Display Unit) (iii) Mouse (iv) light pen (v) Scanner (vi) Joystick (vii) Voice recognizer (viii) Card reader (ix) Digitizer (x) Floppy drive (xi) Tape drive (xii) Cartridge tape drive (xiii) OCR (Optical Character Reader) (xiv) OMR (Optical Mark Reader) etc.

OUTPUT UNIT

Output unit consists of devices with the help of which we get theinformation from computer. Output unit is a link between computer and user. Output devices translate the computer's output into the form understandable by user.

Examples of Output devices:
(i) VDU (ii) Line Printer (iii) Dot matrix printer (iv) Daisy wheel printer (v) Laser printer (vi) Colour graphic terminal (vii) Graph plotter (viii) Floppy drive (ix) Tape drive (x) Disk drive (xi) Cartridge tape drive etc.

ALU(Arithmetic and Logic Unit)

This unit consists of two subsections:
- Arithmetic section
- Logic section

Arithmetic Section: Function of Arithmetic section is to perform arithmetic operations like addition, subtraction, multiplication & division. All complex operation are done by making repetitive use of above operation.

Logic Section: Function of logic section is to perform logic operations such as comparing, selecting, matching and merging of data.

The arithmetic and logic unit (ALU) contains a number of storage locations referred to as registers. These registers are composed of electronic circuitry having the capability of adding, subtracting, multiplying rounding off etc., the number of registers in a computer vary from model to model. However, the basic registers in any computer are the adder and the accumulator.

An interesting side limit is that a computer can only add. It can not carry out subtraction, Multiplication and division operating in the way it is done manually. For these operations, it also has to take the add route. Thus if 15 to be multiplied by 10, the computer adds the data item 15 times. For subtraction and division, it employs the 1's complement method, which again is a form of the addition process. The basic add & subtract operation have been carried out by the computer by means of dedicated circuits called micropragrams.

CONTROL UNIT

Control unit controls the operations of all parts of computers. It does not carry out any actual data processing operations.

- It retrieves instructions from the main memory and determines what is to be taken.
- It then retrieves the data required to be processed from the main memory.
- It causes the CPU to actually carry out required operations and determine whether the required operation have been carried out or not.
- It places the processed results in the output area of the memory.
- It fetches the next instruction from the memory and repeat the whole cycle of operations outlined above.

In addition to the above, the control unit also oversees that erroneous data does not enter into the system (for example, numeric data consisting of alphabets or a number is divided by zero). When such an event occurs, the control unit displays an error on the screen of the CPU to warn computer operator.

In order to carry out these operations, the control unit also has its own set of registers (like those of ALU). The basic register of the control unit are the instruction register, the decoder & the address register.

MEMORY OR STORAGE UNIT

The function of storage unit is to store instruction, data and intermediate results. This unit supplies information to the other units of the computer when needed. It is also known as internal storage unit or main memory or primary storage. Memory is part of the main computer system. The processor access the main memory in direct fashion, that is, the processor can access any location of this memory either to read information from it or store information in it. The primary memory is implemented by two types of memory technologies. The first is called random access memory (RAM) an other is read only memory(ROM). Its size affects speed, power and capabilities.

Random Access Memory

RAM directly provides the required information to the processor. It can be defined as a block of sequential memory locations, each of which has a unique address determining the location and those locations contain a data element. Storage locations in main memory are addressed directly by the CPU's instructions. It is volatile in nature, as soon as powered turned off, the information stored in it will lost. RAM can be further divided into two categories:

- Dynamic Random Access Memory
- Static Random Access Memory

Dynamic Random Access Memory(DRAM):

This type of memory holds the data in dynamic manner with the help of a refresh circuitry. Each second or even less that contents of each memory cell is read and the reading action refreshing the contents of the memory. Due to refreshing action, this memory is called dynamic RAM.

Static Random Access Memory (SRAM):

SRAM along with DRAM is essential for a system to run optimally, because it is very fast as compared to DRAM. It is effective because most programs access the same data repeatedly and keeping all this information in the first written to SRAM assuming that it will be used again soon. SRAM is generally included in computer system by the name of cache.

Read Only Memory (ROM)

As the name suggests, read only memory can only be read, not written. CPU can only read from any location in the ROM but cannot write. The contents of ROM are not lost even in case of a sudden power failure, making it non-volatile in nature. The instructions in ROM are built into the electronic circuit of the chip. These instructions are called firmware. Read only memory is also random access in nature, which means that CPU can randomly access any location within ROM. Improvement in technology for construction flexible ROM has brought, PROM(Programmable Read Only Memory), PROM(Erasable Programmable Read Only Memory), and EEPROM(Electrical Erasable Read Only Memory) into existence.

Cache Memory

Cache is a piece of very fast memory, made from high-speed static RAM that reduces the access time of the data. It is very expensive generally incorporated in the processor, where valuable data and program segments are kept. Main reason for introducing cache in between main memory and processor is to compensate the speed mismatch. Figure shows 1.3 the role of cache in memory-processor communication.

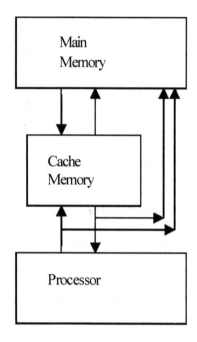

Figure 1.3 Role of Cache in Memory- Processor Communication

Secondary Memory

Secondary storage provides large, non-volatile, and inexpensive storage for programs and data. However, the access time in secondary memory is much larger than in primary memory. Secondary storage permits the storage of computer instructions and data for long periods of time.

Secondary storage is also called auxiliary or bulk memory. Magnetic disks(Hard disks, floppy disks, CD-RW) and magnetic tape are examples of secondary storage.

Hierarchy of memories

* **Internal Processor Memories**

  These consists of set of high-speed registers that are internal to a processor and are used as temporary storage locations to hold data during processing.

* **Primary Memory or Main Memory**

  This memory is large as compared to inter processor memory but not as fast. This memory has direct link with internal processor memory.

• **Secondary Memory or Auxiliary Memory**

This memory is much large in size compared to main memory but is slower.

There is another kind of memory used in modern computers. It is called **cache** memory. Though it is a part of main memory, it is logically positioned between the internal memory, registers, and main memory.

Figure 1.4 shows the hierarchy of memories.

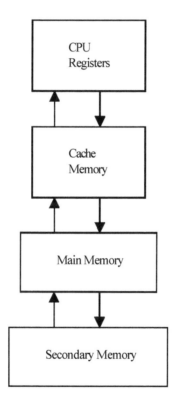

Figure 1.4 The Memory hierarchy

Unit of Memory

The various units used to measure computer memory, are as follows:

Bit: Bit, Abbreviation for **binary digit**, is basic unit of memory. It is smallest unit of information. Bit is represented by a lower case **b.**

Byte: A unit of 8 bits is known as a byte. Hence, a byte is able to contain any binary number between 00000000 and 11111111. It is represented by uppercase **B.**

Kilobyte: One **KB** is equal to 1024 bytes.

****

CHAPTER – 2
Input Devices

Structure
2.0 Objective
2.1 Introduction
2.2. Input Devices
2.2.1 Keyboard
2.2.2 Pointing Devices
       2.2.2.1 Mouse
        2.2.2.2 Trackball
        2.2.2.3 Joystick
        2.2.2.4 Light Pen
        2.2.2.5 Scanners
        2.2.2.6 Optical Scanners

2.0 Objective

A computer accepts (input) information and manipulates (processes) it to get desired result (output) on a sequence of instructions. In the previous lesson, we discussed that a computer system essentially consists of three components: input devices, central processing unit, and output devices. Input devices are used to provide data to the central processing unit for processing. The aim of this lesson is to familiarise you with the various types of input devices along with their advantages, disadvantages, and applications.

2.1 Introduction

Input devices are used to provide data to the central processing unit for processing. After processing, the input data is converted into meaningful information and this output is presented to the user with the help of output devices. In computer terminology devices can be refereed as a unit of hardware, which is capable of providing input to the computer or receiving output or both. An input device captures information and translates into form understandable by computer and output devices(will be discus in lesson number 3) translate information into form understandable by human-being as shown in fig 2.1. Input devices let the user talk to the computer. Output devices let the computer communicate to the user. The common input devices are keyboards and mouse. The output devices are monitors and printers.

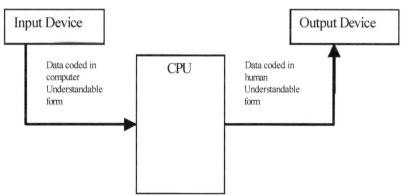

Figure 2.1 Interrelationship between Input device, CPU and Output Device

2.2 Input Devices

Input devices can be broadly classified into the following categories:

2.2.1. Keyboard

2.2.2 Pointing Devices

2.2.3. Speech Recognition

2.2.4. Digital Camera

2.2.5 Scanners

2.2.6. Optical Scanners

2.2.1 Keyboard

Keyboard is designed to resemble a regular typewriter with a few additional keys. A keyboard is the most common data entry device. Using a keyboard, the user can type text and execute commands. Data is entered into computer by simply pressing various keys. The layout of a keyboard come in various styles such as QWERTY, DVORAK, AZERTY but the most common layout is the QWERTY. It is named so because the first six keys on the top row of letters are Q,W E, R, T, and Y. The number of keys on a typical keyboard varies from 82 keys to 108 keys. Portable computers such as laptops quite often have custom keyboards that have slightly different key arrangements than a standard keyboard. In addition, many system manufacturers add special buttons to the standard layout. Keyboard is the easiest input device, as it does not require any special skill, it is supplied with a computer so no additional cost is incurred. The maintenance and operation cost of keyboard is also less. However, using a

keyboard for data entry may be a slow process.

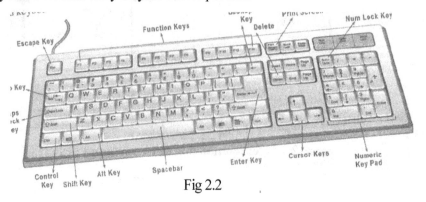

Fig 2.2

12

Layout of the Keyboard

The layout of the keyboard can be divided into the following five sections:

Typing Keys: These keys include the letter keys (1, 2, A, B, etc.), which are generally laid out in the same style that was common for typewriters.

Numeric Keypad: Numeric keys are located on the right hand side of the keyboard. Generally, it consists of a set of 17 keys that are laid out in the same configuration used by most adding machines and calculators.

Function Keys: The functions keys (FI, F2, F3, etc.) are arranged in a row along the top of the keyboard and could be assigned specific commands by the current application or the operating system.

Control Keys: These keys provide cursor and screen control. It includes four directional arrows($\leftarrow \uparrow \rightarrow \downarrow$). These keys allow the user to move the cursor on the display area one space at a time in either an up, down, left or right direction. Control keys also include Home, End, Insert, Delete, Page Up, Page Down, Control (Ctrl), Alternate (A lt), and Escape (Esc).

Special Purpose Keys: Apart from the above-mentioned keys, a keyboard contains some special purpose keys such as Enter, Shift, Caps Lock, Num Lock, Spacebar, Tab, and Print Screen.

Working of a Keyboard

A keyboard is series of switches connected to a small keyboard microprocessor. When the user presses a key, it causes a change in the amount of current flowing through the circuit associated specifically with that key. The keyboard microprocessor detects this change in current flow. By doing this, the processor can tell when a key has been pressed and when it is being released. The processor generates the associative code, known as scan code, of the key and sends it to the operating system. A copy of this code is also stored in the keyboard's memory.

2.2.2 Pointing Devices

In some applications, keyboard is not convenient. For example, if the user wants to select an item from a list, the user can identify that items position by selecting it through the keyboard. However, this action could be performed quickly by pointing at correct position. A pointing device is used to communicate with the computer by pointing to location on the screen. Some of the commonly used pointing devices are **mouse, trackball, joystick, light pen, and touch panel.**

2.2.2.1 Mouse

Mouse is a small hand-held pointing device, which is rectangular-shaped with a rubber ball embedded at its lower side and buttons on the top. Usually a mouse contains two or three buttons, which can be used to input commands or information. Figure 2.3 shows a mouse with three buttons.

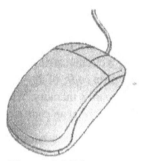

Figure 2.3 Mouse

The mouse may be classified as a mechanical mouse or an optical mouse, based on technology it uses. A mechanical mouse uses a rubber ball at the bottom surface, which rotates as the mouse is moved along a flat surface, to move the cursor. Mechanical mouse is the most common and least expensive pointing device. Microsoft, IBM, and Logitech are some well-known makers of the mechanical mouse.

An optical mouse uses a light beam instead of a rotating ball to detect movement across a specially patterned mouse pad. As the user rolls the mouse on a flat surface, the cursor on the screen also moves in the direction of the mouse's movement.

An optical mouse has the following benefits over the mechanical mouse:

- No moving part means less wear and a lower chance of failure.

- Dirt cannot get inside the mouse and hence no interference with the tracking sensors.
- They do not require a special surface such as a mouse pad.

The cursor of the mouse can be text cursor or graphic cursor. The text cursor(I) is used for text while the graphic cursor( )is used for pointing and drawing.

A mouse allows us to create graphic elements on the screen, such as lines, curves, and freehand shapes. Since it is an intuitive device, it is much easier and convenient to work as compared to the keyboard. Like keyboard, usually it is also supplied with a computer; therefore, no additional cost is incurred. The mouse cannot easily be used with laptop, notebook or palmtop computers. These need a track ball or a touch sensitive pad called a touch pad.

Working of a mouse

A mechanical mouse has a rubber ball in the bottom. When the user moves the mouse, the ball rolls along the surface of the mouse pad, and the mouse keeps track of how far the ball rolls. This allows it to tell how far it has moved. Inside the bottom of the mouse are three rollers. These rollers are mounted at a 90° angle to the one other, one roller measures how fast the ball is turning horizontally, and the other measures how fast it is turning vertically. When the ball rolls, it turns these two rollers. The rollers are connected to axles, and the axles are connected to a small sensor that measures how fast the axle is turning. Both sets of information are passed to the electronics inside the mouse. This little processor, usually consisting of little more than a single chip, uses the information to determine how fast the mouse   itself   is   Processor   Chip   moving,   and   in what direction. This information is passed to the computer via mouse cord, where the operating system then moves the pointer accordingly.

The optical mouse uses an infrared light and special mouse pads with fine grid lines to measure the rotation of the axle. The axle in optical mouse is connected to a little photo-interrupter wheel with a number of tiny holes in it. In front of this wheel is a light and on the other side of the wheel is a light meter. As the wheel turns, the light flashes through the holes in the wheel. By measuring how often these flashes occur, the light sensor can measure how fast the wheel is turning and sends the corresponding coordinates to the computer. The computer moves the cursor on the screen based on the coordinates received from the mouse. This happens hundreds of times each second, making the cursor appear to move very smoothly.

2.2.2.2 Trackball

Trackball is another pointing device that resembles a ball nestled in a square cradle and serves as an alternative to a mouse. In general, a trackball is as if a mouse is turned upside down. It has a ball, which can be rotated by fingers in any direction, the cursor moves accordingly. The size of the ball of the trackball varies from as large as a cue ball, to as small as a marble. Since, it is a static device so rather than rolling the mouse on the top of the table, the ball on the top is moved by using fingers, thumbs, and palms. This pointing device comes in various shapes and forms but with the same functionality. The three shapes, which are commonly used, are a ball, a button, and a square.

2.2.2.3 Joystick

Joystick is a device that moves in all directions and controls the movement of the cursor. The joystick offers three types of control: digital, glide, and direct. Digital control allows movement in a limited number of directions such as up, down, left, and right.

Glide and direct control allow movements in all directions (360 degrees). Direct control joysticks have the added ability to respond to the distance and speed which user moves the stick. A joystick is generally used to control the velocity of the screen cursor movement rather than its absolute position. Joysticks are mainly used for computer games, for other applications, which includes flight simulators, training simulators, CAD/CAM systems, and for controlling industrial robots.

Figure 2.5 Joystick

2.2.2.4 Light Pen

It is the pen like device, which is connected to the machine by a cable. A light pen (sometimes called a mouse pen) is a hand-held electro-optical pointing device which when touched to or aimed closely at a connected computer monitor, will allow the computer to determine where on that screen the pen is aimed. It actually does not emit light; its light sensitive-diode would sense the light coming from the screen. The light coming

17

from the screen causes the photocell to respond by generating a pulse. This electric response is transmitted to the processor that identifies the position to which the light pen is pointing. With the movement of light pen over the screen, the lines or images are drawn.

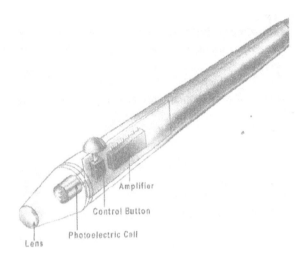

Figure 2.6 Light Pen

It facilitates drawing images and selects objects on the display screen by directly pointing the objects with the pen.

2.2.2.5 Digital Camera

Digital camera stores images digitally rather than recording them on a film. Once a picture has been taken, it can be downloaded to a computer system and then manipulated with an image editing software and printed. The big advantage of digital cameras is that making photos is both inexpensive and fast because there is no film processing.

All digital cameras record images in an electronic form, that is, the image is represented in computer's language, the language of bits and bytes. Essentially, a digital image is just a long string of 1's and 0's that represent all the tiny colored dots or pixels that collectively make up the image. Just like a conventional camera, it has a series of lenses that focus light to create an image of a scene.

Basic difference between digital camera and film-based cameras is that the digital camera does not have a film; it has a sensor that converts light into electrical charges.

2.2.2.6 Scanners

There are a number of situations when some information (picture or text) is available on paper and is needed on the computer disk for further manipulation. The simplest way would be to take a photograph of the image directly from the source and convert it into a form that can be saved on the disk. A scanner scans an image and transforms the image to ASCII codes (the code used by a computer to represent the characters you find on your keyboard - letters of the alphabet, numbers, punctuation marks, etc.) and graphics. These can be edited, manipulated, combined, and then printed. Scanners use a light beam to scan the input data. If the data to be scanned is an image, it can be changed by using the special image editing software. If the image is a page of text, then the special optical character recognition software must be used to covert the images of letters in text and this can be edited by using a word processor.

The two most common types of scanners are hand-held scanner and flat-bed scanner.

Hand-Held Scanner

A hand-held scanner consists of light emitting diodes, which are placed over the material to be scanned. This scanner performs the scanning of the document very slowly from the top to the bottom, with its light on. In this process, all the documents are converted and then stored as an image. While working, the scanner is dragged very steadily and carefully over the document and it should move at a constant speed without stopping, or jerking in order to obtain best results. Due to this reason, hand-held scanners are widely used where high accuracy is not of much importance.

document very slowly from the top to the bottom, with its light on. In this process, all the documents are converted and then stored as an image. While working, the scanner is dragged very steadily and carefully over the document and it should move at a constant speed without stopping, or jerking in order to obtain best results. Due to this reason, hand-held scanners are widely used where high accuracy is not of much importance.

The size of the hand-held scanners is

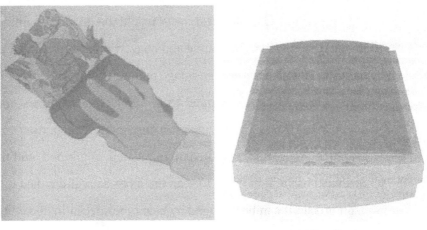

(a) Hand-held scanner　　　　　　　**(b) Flat-Bed scanner**

Figure 2.7

small shown in fig 2.7(a). They come in various resolutions, up to about 800 dpi (dots per inch) and are available in either grey scale or colour.

Flat-Bed Scanner

Flat-bed scanners look similar to a photocopier machine. It consists of a box containing a glass plate on its top and a lid that covers the glass plate. This glass plate is primarily used for placing the document to be scanned. The light beam is placed below the glass plate and when it is activated, it moves from left to right horizontally. After scanning one line, the beam of light moves in order to scan the next line and thus, the procedure is repeated until all the lines are scanned. For scanning, an A4 size document takes about 20 seconds. These scanners are capable of scanning black and white as well as colour images. The flat-bed scanners are larger in size and more expensive than the hand-held scanners shown in fig. 2.7(b).

However, they usually produce better quality images because they employ better scanning technology.

2.2.2.7 Optical Scanners

There are four types of optical recognition: optical character recognition (OCR), optical mark recognition (OMR), magnetic ink character recognition (MICR), and bar code reader.

Optical Character Recognition (OCR)

Optical Character Recognition (OCR) is a process of scanning printed pages as images on a flatbed scanner and then using OCR software to recognise the letters as ASCII text. The OCR software has tools for both acquiring the image from a scanner and recognising the text. In the OCR system, a book or a magazine article is fed directly into an electronic computer file, and then this file is edited by using a word processor. Advanced OCR systems can read text in a large variety of fonts, but they still have difficulty with handwritten text. OCR works best with originals or very clear copies and mono-spaced fonts like Courier.

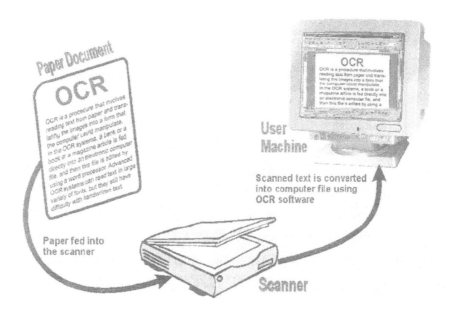

Figure 2.8 OCR System

Optical Mark Recognition (OMR)

Optical Mark Recognition (OMR) is the process of detecting the presence of intended marked responses. A mark registers significantly less light than the surrounding paper. Optical mark reading is done by a special device known as optical mark reader. The OMR technology enables a high speed reading of large quantities of data and transferring this data to computer without using a keyboard. The OMR reader scans the form, detects the presence of marks, and passes this information to the computer for processing by application software. Generally, this technology is used to read answer sheets (objective type tests). In this method, special printed forms/documents are printed with boxes, which can be marked with dark pencil or ink. These forms are then passed under a light source and the presence of dark ink is transformed into electric pulses, which are transmitted to the computer.

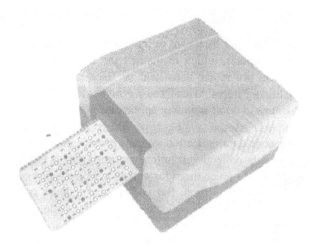

Figure 2.9 Optical Mark Recognition

Optical mark recognition is also used for standardized testing as well as course enrolment and attendance in education.

OMR has a better recognition rate than OCR because fewer mistakes are made by machines to read marks than in reading handwritten characters. Large volumes of data can be collected quickly and easily without the need for specially trained staff. Usually, an OMR reader can maintain a throughput of 1500 to 10000 forms per hour. It requires accurate alignment of printing on forms and need a paper of good quality.

Optical mark recognition is traditionally performed using reflective light method where a beam of light is reflected on a sheet with marks, to capture the reflection (presence of mark) or absence of reflection (absence of mark).

Magnetic-Ink Character Recognition (MICR)

Specifically, it refers to the special magnetic encoding, printed on the bottom of a negotiable check. This information is machine readable via bank reader/sorters, which read the visual patterns and magnetic waveforms of the MICR encoding.

The characters are printed using special ink, which contains iron particles that can be magnetised. Magnetic ink character readers are used generally in banks to process the cheques. In case of bank cheques, the numbers written at the bottom are recorded in MICR (using special magnetic ink), representing unique cheque numbers, bank, and branch code, etc. A MICR reads these characters by examining their shapes in a matrix form and the information is then passed on to the computer.

Figure 2.11 Magnetic-Ink Character Recognition

The banking industry prefers MICR because as compared to the OCR, it gives extra security against forgeries such as colour copies of payroll cheques or hand-altered characters on a cheque. The reading speed of the MICR is also higher. This method is very efficient and time saving for data processing.

Bar Code Reader

Bar code is a machine-readable code in the form of a pattern of parallel vertical lines of varying widths. They are commonly used for labelling goods that are available in super markets, numbering books in libraries, etc. These codes/stripes are sensed and read by a photoelectric device (bar code reader) that reads the code by means of reflective light. The information recorded in bar code reader is then fed into the computer, which recognises the information from the thickness and spacing of bars. Bar code readers are either hand-held or fixed-mount. Hand-held scanners are used to read bar codes on stationary items. With fixed-mount scanners, items having a bar code are passed by the scanner - by hand as in retail scanning applications or by conveyor belt in many industrial applications. A bar code scanner can record data five to seven times faster than a skilled typist can record. A bar code data entry has an error rate of about I in 3 million. Bar coding also reduces cost in terms of labour and reduced revenue losses resulting from data collection errors.

Figure 2.12 Hand-held bar code reader
****

CHAPTER – 3
OUTPUT DEVICES

3.0 Objective

3.1 Introduction

3.2 Classification of Output Devices

    3.2.1 Hardcopy Devices

        3.2.1.1 Impact Printers

        3.2.1.2 Non-Impact Printers

        3.2.1.3 Plotters

    3.2.2. Softcopy Devices

        3.2.2.1 Monitors

        3.2.2.2 Projectors

        3.2.2.3 Audio Output

3.3 Terminal

3.0 Objective

A computer accepts (input) information and manipulates (processes) it to get desired result (output) on a sequence of instructions. In the previous lesson, we have discussed various types of input devices used to provide data to the central processing unit for processing. The aim of this lesson is to familiarize you with the various types of output devices to get desired result that may be in various form viz text, graphics, audio, and video; along with their advantages, disadvantages, and applications.

3.1 Introduction

Output devices convert machine-readable information into human-readable form. The basic functioning of output devices is just the opposite of the input devices, that is, the data is 'fed into' the computer system through the input devices while the output is 'taken out' from the computer through the output devices. However, the output, which comes out from CPU, is in the form of digital signals. The output devices display the processed information by converting them into human-readable form in graphical, alphanumeric or audio-visual forms.

3.2 Classification of Output Devices

Output is data that has been processed into a useful form called information. It can be displayed or viewed on a monitor, printed on a printer, or listened through speakers or a headset.

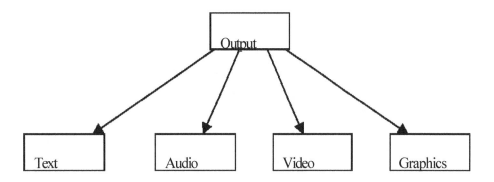

Figure 3.1 Types of Output

There are four basic areas of the output devices:

Text: Textual form of output consists of characters (letters, numbers, punctuation marks, or any other symbol requiring one byte of computer storage space) that are used to create words, sentences, and paragraphs. Graphics: Graphics are digital representations of non-text information such as drawings, charts, photographs, and animation (a series of still images in sequence that gives the illusion of motion).

Audio: Audio includes music, speech or any sound. A computer converts the sound from a continuous analog signal into a digital format. Most output devices require the computer to convert digital format back into analog signals.

Video: Video consists of images that are played back at speed that provide the illusion of full motion. The images are often captured with a video input device like a video camera. A video capture card is required to convert an analog video signal into a digital signal that the computer can understand. Some output devices accept the digital signal, while others convert the digital signals into analog signals.

The outputs, which can be easily understood and used by human beings, are of following two forms:

1. Hard Copy: The physical form of output is known as hard copy. Ingeneral, it refers to the recorded information copied from a computer onto paper or some other durable surface, such as microfilm. Hard copy output is permanent and relatively stable form of output. This type of output is also highly portable. Paper is one of the most widely used hard copy output media. The principal examples are printouts, whether text or graphics, from printers. Film, including microfilm and microfiche, is also considered as a hard copy output.

2 Soft Copy: The electronic version of an output, which usually resides in computer memory and or on disk, is known as soft copy. Unlike hard copy, soft copy is not a permanent form of output. It is transient and is usually displayed on the screen. This kind of output is not tangible, that is, it cannot be touched. Soft copy output includes audio and visual form of output, which is generated using a computer. In addition, textual or graphical information displayed on a computer monitor is also a soft copy form of output.

Hard copy devices are very slow in operation as compared to the soft copy devices.

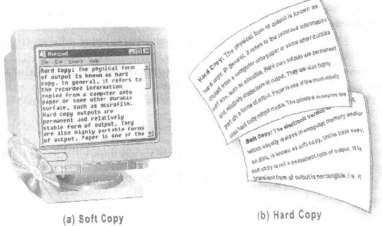

(a) Soft Copy   (b) Hard Copy

Figure 3.2 Two types of outputs

Based on the hard copy and soft copy outputs, the output devices are classified into two types: hard copy output devices and soft copy output devices.

3.2.1 Hard Copy Output devices

Among the wide variety of the hard copy output devices, printers, and plotters are the most commonly used. A printer is used to produce printouts of the documents stored on a computer's disk drive. A plotter is a pen-based output device, which is used for producing high quality output by moving ink pens across the paper.

3.21.2 Impact Printers

As their names specify, impact printers work by physically striking a head or needle against an ink ribbon to make a mark on the paper. Impact printers are the oldest printing technology and are still in use. An impact printers can print only one character at a time while some impact printers can print an entire line. The three most commonly used impact printers are dot matrix printers, daisy wheel printers, and drum printers.

Characteristics of impact printers

- In impact printers, there is physical contact with the paper to produce an image.
- They have relatively low consumable costs. The primary recurring costs for these printers are the ink ribbons and paper.
- Due to being robust and low cost, they are useful for bulk printing.
- They can withstand dusty environment, vibrations, and extreme temperature.
- Impact printers are ideal for printing multiple copies (that is, carbon copies) because they can easily print through many layers of paper.
- Due to its striking activity, impact printers are very noisy.
- Since they are mechanical in nature, they tend to be slow.
- Impact printers do not support transparencies.

Dot matrix printers

Dot matrix printer (also known as the wire matrix printer) is the oldest printing technology and it prints one character at a time. Usually, dot matrix printers can print any shape of character, which a user can specify. This allows the printer to print many special characters, different sizes of print, and enables it to print graphics, such as charts and graphs. The speed of dot matrix printers is measured in characters per second (cps). Most dot matrix printers offer different speeds depending on the quality of print desired. The speed can vary from about 200 to over 500 cps. The print quality is determined by the number of pins (the mechanisms that print the dots), which can vary from 9 to 24. The more pins per inch, the higher the print resolution. The best dot matrix printers (24 pins) can produce near letter quality type image. Most dot matrix printers have a resolution ranging from 72-360 dpi.

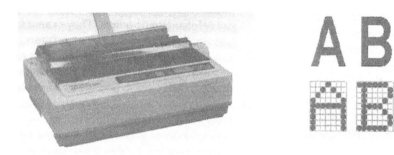

(a) Dot Matrix Printer   **(b) Dot Matrix characters**

Figure 3.3

Dot matrix printers are inexpensive and have low operating costs. These printers are able to use different types of fonts, different line densities, and different types of paper. Many dot matrix printers are bi-directional, that is, they can print the characters from direction, left or right. The major limitation of dot matrix printer is that it prints only in black and white. The image printing ability is also very limited. These printers may not be able to print graphic objects adequately but can handle applications such as accounting, personnel, and payroll very well. Dot matrix printers are commonly used in low-cost, low-quality applications like cash registers. These printers are limited to situations where carbon copies are needed and the quality is not too important.

Working of a dot matrix printer

The technology behind dot matrix printing is quite simple. The paper is pressed against a drum (a rubber-coated cylinder) and is intermittently pulled forward as printing progresses. The printer consists of an electro-magnetically driven print head, which is made up of numerous print wires (pins). The characters are formed by moving the electro-magnetically driven print head across the paper, which strikes the printer ribbon situated between the paper and print head pin. As the head stamps onto the paper through the inked ribbon, a character is produced that is made up of these dots. These dots seem to be very small for the normal vision and appear like solid human readable characters.

Daisy wheel printers

It is named so because the print head of this printer resembles a daisy flower, with the printing arms that appear like the petals of the flower. These printers are commonly referred to as letter quality printers as the print quality is as good as that of a high-quality typewriter.

Daisy wheel printers produce high-resolution output and are more reliable than dot matrix printers. They can have speeds up to 90 cps. These printers are also called as smart printers because of its bidirectional printing and built-in microprocessor control features.

Figure 3.4 Daisy Wheel Printer

However, daisy wheel printers give only alphanumeric output. They cannot print graphics and cannot change fonts unless the print wheel is physically replaced: These printers are usually very slow because of the time required to rotate the print wheel for each character desired. Daisy wheel printers are slower and more expensive than dot matrix printers.

Working of a daisy wheel printer

These printers have print heads composed of metallic or plastic wheels. A raised character is placed on the tip of each of the daisy wheels 'petals'. Each petal has an appearance of a letter (upper case and lower case), number or punctuation mark on it. To print, the print wheel is rotated around until the desired character is under the print hammer. The petal is then struck from behind by the print hammer, which strikes the character, pushing it against the ink ribbon, and onto the paper, creating the character.

Drum printers

Such types of printers print an entire line in a single operation. Such printers are known as line printers. Drum printer is one of the most commonly used line printers. This arrangement allows a continuous high- speed printing. Its printing speed varies from 150 lines to 2500 lines per minute with 96 to 160 characters on a 15-inch line. Although, such printers are much faster than character printers, they tend to be quite loud, have limited multi-font capability, and often produce lower print quality than most recent printing technologies. Line printers are designed for heavy printing applications. For example, in businesses where enormous amounts of materials are printed.

Figure 3.5 Drum Printer

Working of a drum printer

The basics of a line printer like drum printer are similar to those of a serial printer, except that multiple hammers strike multiple type elements against the paper almost simultaneously, so that an entire line is printed in one operation. A typical arrangement of a drum printer involves a large rotating drum mounted horizontally and positioned in front of a very wide, inked ribbon, which in turn is positioned in front of the paper itself. The drum contains characters molded onto its surface in columns around its circumference; each column contains a complete set of characters (letters, digits, etc.) running around the circumference of the drum. The drum spins continuously at high speed when the printer is operating. In order to print a line, hammers positioned behind the paper ram the paper against the ribbon and against the drum beyond it at exactly the right instant; such that the appropriate character is printed in each column as it spins past on the drum. Once every column has been printed, the paper is advanced upward so that the next line can be printed.

3.1.1.2 Non-Impact Printers

Unlike impact printers, a non-impact printer forms characters and images without making direct physical contact between printing mechanism and paper. In this printer, the print head does not make contact with the paper, and no inked ribbon is required. Ink can be sprayed against the paper and then heat and pressure are used to fuse a fine black powder into the shape of a character. They use techniques other than physically striking the page to transfer ink onto the page. The major technologies competing in the non-impact market are ink-jet and laser.

Characteristics of non-impact printers

- Non-impact printers are faster than impact printers.
- They are quieter than impact printers because there is no striking mechanism involved and only few moving parts are used.
- They possess the ability to change typefaces automatically.
- These printers produce high-quality graphics.

33

- These printers usually support the transparencies.
- These printers cannot print multipart forms because no impact is being made on the paper.

Ink-Jet Printer

It is the most type of printer used in home. Being a non-impact it does not touches the paper while creating an image. It uses a series of nozzles to spay onto the paper. Originally it was made black and white only. However, the print head has now been expanded and the nozzle accommodates CMYK. The combination of these four colors will be the resultant color.

Figure 3.6 Ink-Jet Printer

These printers are costlier than the dot matrix printers, but the quality is much better. Ink-jet printers typically print with a resolution of 600 dpi or more. Due to the high resolution, these printers produce high quality graphics and text printouts. They are also affordable, which appeals to small businesses and home offices. These printers print documents at a medium pace, but slow down if printing a document with multicolor. These printers can print about 6 pages a minute. Moreover, they can also be programmed to print unusual symbols such as Japanese or Chinese characters.

Working of an ink-jet printer

An ink-jet printer has a print cartridge with a series of tiny electrically heated chambers. These cartridges are attached to print heads with a series of small nozzles that spray ink onto the surface of the paper. As print head moves back and forth across the page, software gives instructions regarding the type and the quantity of colors. It also tells the position where the dots of ink should be 'sprayed'. There are two main ways to drop the ink droplets, namely, the bubble-jet and piezo-electric technology.

Bubble-jet printers use heat to fire ink onto the paper. Piezo-electric technology uses a piezo crystal at the back of the ink reservoir.

Laser printers

A laser printer provides the highest quality text and images for personal computers today, operates on the same principle as that of a photocopy machine. They are also known as page printers because they process and store the entire page before they actually print it.

Characteristics of Laser printer

- It is a very fast printer.
- It can print text and graphics with a very high quality resolution from 300 to 1200 dpi.
- It can print in different fonts, that is, type styles and sizes.
- It is more expensive to buy and maintain than the other printers.

Figure 3.7 Laser Printer

Working of a laser printer

The core component of laser printing system is the photoreceptor drum. A rotating mirror inside the printer causes the beam of a laser to sweep across the photoconductive drum. Initially, the beam of laser charges the photoconductive drum positively. When the charged photoconductor is exposed to an optical image through a beam of light to discharge, a latent or invisible image is formed. At the point where the laser strikes the surface of drum, it creates a dot of positive charge. These points are represented by a black dot, which will be printed on the paper. After this, the printer coats the drum with a container, which contains a black powder called toner. This toner is negatively charged, and so it clings to the positive areas of the drum surface. When the powder pattern gets fixed, the drum is rotated and the paper is fed into the drum surface via a pressure roller. This pressure roller transfers the black toner onto the paper. Since the paper is moving at the same speed as the drum, the paper picks up the image pattern precisely. Finally, the printer passes the paper through the fuser, a pair of heated rollers. As the paper passes through these rollers, the loose toner powder gets melted and fuses with the fibers in the paper.

3.2.1.3 Plotters

A plotter is a pen-based output device that is attached to a computer for making vector graphics, that is, images created by a series of many straight lines. It is used to draw high-resolution charts, graphs, blueprints, maps, circuit diagrams, and other line-based diagrams. Plotters are similar to printers, but they draw lines using a pen. As a result, they can produce continuous lines, whereas printers can only simulate lines by printing a closely spaced series of dots. Multicolor plotters use different-colored pens to draw different colors. Color plots can be made by using four pens (cyan, magenta, yellow, and black) and need no human intervention to change them.

Plotters are relatively expensive as compared to printers but can produce more printouts than standard printers. They are mainly used for Computer Aided Design (CAD) and Computer Aided Manufacturing (CAM) applications such as printing out plans for houses or car parts. These are also used with programs like AUTO CAD (computer assisted drafting) to give graphic outputs.

Types of Plotters

There are two different types of plotters, one where the paper moves (drum), and the other where the paper is stationary (flatbed plotter).

Drum Plotters: In drum plotters, the paper on which the design is to be made is placed over a drum. These plotters consist of one or more pen(s) that are mounted on a carriage and this carriage is horizontally placed across the drum. The drum can rotate in either clockwise or anticlockwise direction under the control of plotting instructions sent by the computer. Drum plotters are used to produce continuous output, such as plotting earthquake activity, or for long graphic output, such as tall building structures.

Flatbed Plotters: Flatbed plotters consist of a stationary horizontal plotting surface on which paper is fixed. The pen is mounted on a carriage, which can move horizontally, vertically, leftwards or rightwards to draw line. In flatbed plotters, the paper does not move, the pen-holding mechanism provides all the motion. These plotters are instructed by the computer on the movement of pens in the X- Y coordinates on the page. These plotters are capable of working on any standard, that is, from A4 size paper to some very big beds. Depending on the size of the flatbed surface, these are used in designing of ships, aircrafts, buildings, etc. The major disadvantage of this plotter is that it is a slow output device and can take hours to complete a complex drawing.

(a) Drum Plotter

(a) Flatbed Plotter

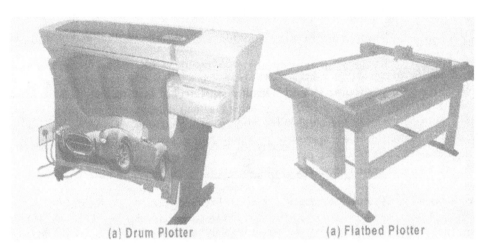

(a) Drum Plotter   (a) Flatbed Plotter

Figure 3.8 Plotters

3.2.2 Soft Copy Output Devices

The devices, which are used for creating the soft copy output, are known as soft copy output devices. Some commonly used soft copy outputs are visual display, audio response and projection display.

3.2.2.1 Monitors

The monitor is the most frequently used soft copy output device. A computer screen, that is, monitor, is TV like display attached to the computer on which the output can be displayed and viewed. The computer screen can be either a monochrome display or a color display. A monochrome screen uses only one colour (usually white, green, amber or black) to display text on contrasting background.

It is the most popular input/output device used with modern computers.

Monitors are available in various sizes like 14, 15, 17, 19, and 21 inches. Notebook computer screen sizes are usually smaller, typically ranging from 12 to 15 inches. Like televisions, screen sizes are normally measured diagonally (in inches), the distance from one corner to the opposite corner.

Raster scan display Raster scan display is the most common type of graphics monitor employed in a CRT. In this system, the electron beam is swept across the screen, one row at a time from top to bottom. As the electron beam moves across each row, the beam intensity is turned ON and OFF to create a pattern of illuminated spots. The picture definition is stored in a memory area called the refresh buffer or frame buffer, which holds the set of intensity values for all the screen points.

Normally, refreshing on raster scan displays is carried out at the rate of 60(60Hz) to 80 (80Hz) frames per second. At the end of each scan line, the electron beam returns to the left side of the screen to begin displaying the next scan line. The return to the left of the screen, after refreshing each scan line, is called the horizontal retrace of the electron beam. At the end of each frame, the electron beam returns to the top left corner of the screen to begin the next frame. This is known as vertical retrace.

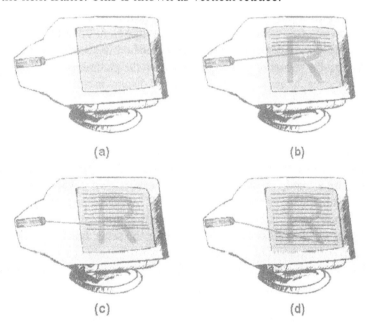

(a)   (b)

(c)   (d)

Figure 3.9 Raster Scan Display

Random scan display

In random scan display system, a CRT has the electron beam directed only to the parts of the screen where a picture is to be drawn. Random scan monitors draw a picture one line at a time and for this reason are referred

39

to as vector displays, stroke-writing or calligraphic displays. The component lines of a picture can be drawn and refreshed by a random scan system in any specified order. Refresh rate on a random scan system depends on the number of lines to be displayed. Picture definition is stored as a set of line drawing commands in an area of memory referred to as the refresh display file (also known as display list, display program, or simply refresh buffer).

Random scan systems are designed for line drawing applications and cannot display realistic shaded scenes. Since picture definition is stored as a set of line drawing instructions and not as a set of intensity values for all screen points, vector displays generally have higher resolution than raster systems. Moreover, vector displays produce smooth line drawings because the CRT beam directly follows the line path.

Color Display on a CRT

A CRT monitor displays color pictures by using a combination of phosphors that emit different colored light. The two basic techniques for producing color displays with a CRT are the beam penetration method and the shadow-mask method.

Beam penetration

In this system, two layers of phosphor (usually red and green) are coated on the inner side of the CRT screen. The displayed color depends on how far the electron beam penetrates into the phosphor layers. A beam of slow electrons excites only the outer red layer while a beam of very fast electrons penetrates through the red layer and excites the inner green layer. At intermediate beam speeds, combinations of red and green light are emitted to show two additional colors, orange and yellow. The speed of the electrons, and hence the screen color at any point, is controlled by the beam-acceleration voltage. The beam-penetration method for displaying colour pictures is commonly used with random scan displays.

However, only four colors are possible, and the quality of pictures is not as good as compared to other methods. Beam penetration is an inexpensive way to produce color on random scan monitors.

Shadow masking

A shadow-mask CRT has three phosphor color dots at each pixel position. One phosphor dot emits a red light, another emits a green light, and the third emits a blue light. This type of CRT has three electron guns, one for each color dot, and a shadow-mask grid just behind the phosphor-coated screen. The three electron beams are deflected and focused as a group onto the shadow mask, which contains a series of holes aligned with the phosphor-dot patterns. When the three beams pass through a hole in the shadow mask, they activate a dot triangle, which appears as a small colour spot on the screen. The phosphor dots in the triangles are arranged so that each electron beam can activate only its corresponding color dot when it passes through the shadow mask.

Color variations in a shadow-mask CRT can be obtained by varying the intensity levels of the three electron beams. For example, a white (or grey) area is the result of activating all three dots with equal intensity.

Shadow-mask method is commonly used in raster scan systems; they produce a much wider range of colors than the beam-penetration method.

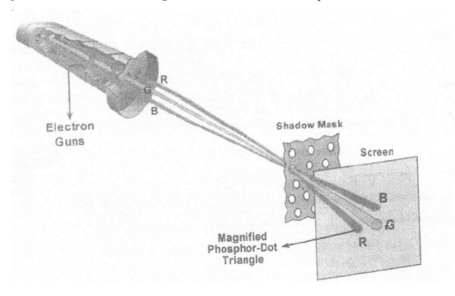

Figure 3.11 Shadow Mask

41

3.2.2.2 Projectors

Screen image projector is an output device, which is used to project information from a computer on to a large screen, so that it can be simultaneously viewed by a large group of people. Projection display is commonly used for classrooms training or conference room or for multimedia presentations with a large audience. Like monitors, projectors provide a temporary, soft copy output.

Types of Projectors

Projectors are mainly of two types:

¾   **LCD Projectors**

LCD is the acronym for Liquid Crystal Display. It is the established technology used by most of the leading manufacturers. Most of today's LCD projectors contain three separate LCD glass panels, one each for red, green, and blue components of the image signal being fed into the projector. As light passes through the LCD panels, individual pixels can be opened to allow light to pass, or closed to block the light. This activity modulates the light and produces the image that is projected onto the screen.

¾   **DLP Projectors**

DLP is the acronym for Digital Light Processing. It is a proprietary technology developed by Texas Instruments. DLP uses a single Digital Mirror Device (DMD) chip that has thousands of tiny mirrors, each representing a single pixel. These mirrors tilt back and forth, directing the light either into the lens path to turn the pixel ON, or away from the lens path to turn it OFF and create the image. DLP is a newer technology than LCD and is used on some of the smallest, lightest projectors currently available. DLP projectors handle video images extremely well.

LCD versus DLP

- LCD controls red, green, and blue independently through three separate LCD panels. As a result, the user can adjust the brightness and contrast of each color channel individually. In most single chip DLP projectors, color is fixed

- LCD delivers a sharper image than DLP at any given resolution. However, it does not mean that DLP is fuzzy.

- LCD is more light-efficient. LCD projectors produce significantly higher lumen outputs than DLP projectors do with the same wattage lamp.

- The DLP light engine consists of a single chip rather than three LCD panels. Hence, DLP projectors tend to be more compact.

3.2.2.3 Audio Output

In the input devices, we have discussed that voice (in speech recognition) can be taken as an input by the computer system. Similarly, the computer can also give output in the form of audio. Audio response is an output media, which produces either verbal or audio responses from the computer system. These sounds are pre-recorded in computer system. Each sound has a unique code.

There are two basic approaches to getting a computer to talk. The first is synthesis by analysis, in which the device analyses the input of an actual human voice speaking words, stores, and processes the spoken sounds, and reproduces them as needed. The second approach to synthesising speech is synthesis by rule, in which the device applies a complex set of linguistic rules to create artificial speech. Synthesis based on the human voice has the advantage of sounding more natural, but it is limited to the number of words stored in the computer.

The standard computer system can provide audio output with the addition of two components: a speech synthesizer that does the speaking and a screen reading software that tells the synthesizer what to say. voice output has become common in many places like airline, bus terminals, banks.

3.3 Terminals

Computer terminal is a special unit that can perform both input and output. It is sometimes called as display terminals or video display terminals (VDTs). Generally, different types of terminals are used in different working areas.

Terminals can be categorized into the following types:

Dumb Terminal: It refers to a terminal that has no processing or programming capabilities. Generally, dumb terminals are used for simple data entry or retrieval tasks. An example of a dumb terminal is the type used by airline clerks at airport ticket and check-in counters.

Smart Terminal: An intelligent terminal has built-in processing capability and memory but does not have its own storage capacity. They are often found in local area networks in offices.

Intelligent Terminal: An intelligent terminal has memory and a processor, that is, it has inbuilt microprocessors, therefore, it is also known as a user-programmable terminal. Personal computers that function as intelligent terminals are basically connected to switch boxes. The intelligent terminals allow them to operate as personal computers or to access a mainframe. This terminal can independently perform a certain number of jobs without even interacting with the mainframe.

****

CHAPTER – 4
Storage Devices

Structure

4.0 Objective

4.1 Introduction

4.2 Primary Memory

    4.2.1 Random Access Memory

    4.2.2 Read Only Memory

4.3 Secondary Memory

    4.3.1 Magnetic Tape

    4.3.2 Magnetic Disk

    4.3.3 Optical Disk

4.0 Objective

The most essential part of computer processing is the memory. From the moment the computer is turned ON until the time it is shut down, the CPU constantly uses memory. CPU requires memory to handle the intermediate results and to store final output. This lesson introduces two broad categories of memories- primary memory and secondary memory, and discusses various types of primary memories and various types of secondary memories with their storage organisation.

4.1 Introduction

Memory refers to the electronic storage place for data and instruction where CPU can access quickly. Thus, CPU requires memory to handle the intermediate results and to store final output. Computer memory is extremely important to computer operation. Files and programs are loaded into memory from external media like hard disk. RAM is the hardware location in a computer where the operating system, application programs, and data in current use are kept so that they can be quickly reached by the computer's processor. RAM is much faster to read from and write to than most other kinds of storage in a computer (like hard disk and floppy disk).

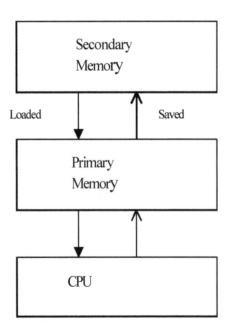

Figure 4.1 Interrelationship of CPU, Primary memory, Secondary memory

The following terms are used to identify the comparative behavior of different types of memory devices and technologies:

Storage Capacity: Storage capacity refers to the size of the memory. The capacity of the internal processor memory is expressed in terms of number of bytes and kilobytes.

Cost: The cost of a memory is valued by estimating the cost per bit of storage, that is, the cost of a storage unit for a given storage capacity. Note that, even though a 40GB hard disk may cost more than 128MB RAM chip, but on comparing the cost with storage space (cost per bit of storage), one will notice that a RAM chip is costlier than a hard disk. Obviously, a lower cost memory is desirable.

Access Mode: The information from memory can be accessed in the following ways: Random: Random access indicates that locations in the memory can be accessed, that is, written or read, in any order regardless of the memory location that was accessed before. RAM and hard disk are the examples of random access memories.

Sequential: In this mode, memory is accessed in predefined sequential order. Magnetic tape is an example of sequential mode.

Direct: In some cases, data is accessed neither in random fashion nor in a sequential fashion, but is a combination of both modes. A separate read/write head exists for a track, and on a track, the information can be accessed sequentially. This type of semi-random mode exists in the magnetic disk.

Physical Characteristic: The physical characteristic of a memory device can be categorised into four parts, namely, electronic, magnetic, mechanical, and optical. One of the important requirements of the storage device is that it should exhibit two physical states, 0 or 1. The access time of the memory depends upon how quickly the state can be recognized and changed. Obviously, the quicker the device recognises the state, the faster it will be.

Permanence of Storage: Some memories retain information for longer duration while others are used to store information for very short period. There are memories, which require constant refreshing to preserve the information; these memories are called dynamic memory. These memories are volatile in nature and loose contents on power failure. Another memory, which retains data forever, is called static memory. This memory comes under a non-volatile category. A non-volatile memory is desirable.

4.2 Primary Memory

Such memories have direct interaction with CPU, due to the named as primary memory. Therefore, the access time for such memories is less as compared to secondary memories.

4.2.1 Random Access Memory (RAM)

It is the place in a computer where the operating system, application programs, and data in current use are kept so that they can be accessed quickly by the computer's processor. RAM is much faster to read from and write to than the other kinds of storage in a computer like the hard disk or floppy disk. However, the data in RAM stays there only as long as the computer is running. When the computer is turned off, RAM loses its data. That is why you need to continuously save the information to the hard disk. RAM can be embedded into a system board, but it is more typically attached to the system board in the form of a chip.

Random access memory is also called read/write memory because, unlike read only memory(ROM) that does not allow any write operation. Random access memory allows CPU to read as well as write data and instructions.

RAM's access time varies from 9 to 70 nanoseconds, depending upon its type. The lesser the nanoseconds, the better the access. The bit size of a CPU displays how many bytes of information it can access from RAM at the same time. For example, a 32-bit CPU can process 4 bytes at a time whereas a 64-bit CPU can process 8 bytes at a time.

RAM is small, both in physical size and for data it can hold. It is much smaller than the hard disk. RAM is available in the capacity of 16, 32, 64, 128, and 256 megabytes, usually increasing in multiples of 8 megabytes. Nowadays, a typical computer may come with 128 megabytes of RAM.

Main Memory Organisation

The main memory is made up of a series of consecutive memory cells, each of which is indexed by a unique number, the address. Information stored in these cells is in the form of fixed number of bits, called as word length. The main memory of computer system is organized into an array of such numerous cells, which are serially link together. The selected memory address can contain one or more bits. However, for speed and practicality, for a given computer design, the word size typically relates to the CPU and is usually the size of its registers in bits. Word sizes typically range in increments of 8, 16, 32 or 64 bits and hence computers are termed as 8-bit, 16-bit, 32-bit or 64-bit computers. The more the number of bits per word, the faster the electronic signal will flow. Hence, the computer will work faster.

Address	Data Stored in Memory Cells(-bit)
1000.	0101 0110
1001.	0101 0100
1002.	0101 0101
1003.	0101 0100
1004.	0101 0101
1005.	0111 0100
1006.	0111 0110

Figure 4.5 Main Memory with 8-bit Word length

The addresses in the memory are assigned in a successive manner, running from initial address location to the largest address location. For example, if the main memory has 256 locations, then the address ranges from 0 to 255. The microprocessor performs read/write operations on the data values by referencing to their corresponding addresses. To find the contents in a cell, the RAM controller sends the column/row address through a very thin electrical line engraved into the chip. There is an address line(Memory Address Register-MAR) and data line(Memory Buffer Register-MBR) for each row and column in the set of cells. If data is being read, the bits that are read flow back on a separate data line. The processor gets the address of RAM location from which data is to be read. This address is sent to the RAM controller. The RAM controller organises the request and sends it down on appropriate address lines, the transistors along the address lines open up the cells so that each capacitor value can be read, in the form of high-value (1) and low-value (0). The entire lines of data are then transmitted along the data lines to the processor's data buffer (cache memory).

Types of RAM

Random access memory is of two types:

Static RAM: This RAM retains the data as long as power is provided to the memory chips. It does not need to be 'refreshed' (pulse of current through all the memory cells) periodically. SRAM is very fast but much more expensive than DRAM. SRAM is often used as cache memory due to its high speed. This type of SRAM can operate at bus speeds higher than 66MHz, so is often used.

Dynamic RAM: DRAM, unlike SRAM, must be continually 'refreshed' in order for it to maintain the data. This is done by placing the memory on a refresh circuit that rewrites the data several hundred times per second. DRAM is used for most system memory because it is cheap and small. DRAM is slower, less expensive and covers less space on computer's motherboard. A typical DRAM may cover one-fourth or even less the silicon area of SRAM.

4.2.2 Read Only Memory (ROM)

A computer system needs special instructions every time during a login operation. This process is required because during login, main memory of the computer is empty due to its volatile property, so there must be some sort of instruction (special boot programs) to be stored in the special chips, which enables the computer system to perform start operations and transfer the control to the operating system.

This special chip, where initial start up instructions is stored, is called ROM (Read Only Memory) chip or non-volatile memory. This non-volatile memory not only performs read operations but restrict themselves to be altered and, therefore, making it much safer and secure than RAM. ROM chips are not only used in the computer but in other electronic items like washing machine and microwave oven. Generally, designers program ROM chips at the time of manufacturing circuits. Programming is done by burning appropriate electronic fuses to form patterns of binary information.

Interaction between RAM, ROM, and CPU

A typical scenario is listed below:

Step 1: The computer is switched ON.

Step 2: Computer loads data from ROM and checks whether all the major components like processor and hard disk are functioning properly.

Step 3: Computer loads BIOS (basic input/output system) from ROM to determine the machine's fundamental configuration and environment. The information stored in ROM BIOS chip determines what peripherals the system can support.

Step 4: Computer loads the operating system from the secondary storage (hard disk) into RAM. This allows the CPU to have immediate access to the operating system, which enhances the performance and functionality of the overall system.

Step 5: When an application is opened, it is loaded into RAM and any file that is opened for use in that application is also loaded into RAM.

Step 6: After processing, when the user saves the file and closes the respective application, the file is written to the specified secondary storage device. After that, the file(s) and the application are 'flushed out' from the RAM.

Types of ROM

Memories in the ROM family are distinguished by the methods used to write new data to them and the number of times they can be rewritten. ROMs come in following varieties:

Masked ROM: The very first ROMs were hard-wired devices that contained a pre-programmed set of data or instructions. These kinds of ROMs are known as masked ROMs. The contents of such ROMs have to be specified before chip production, so the actual data could be used to arrange the transistors inside the chip.

Programmable ROM (PROM): Blank PROM chips can be bought economically and coded by anyone with a special tool such as PROM-programmers. However, once a PROM has been programmed, its contents can never be changed. Creating a ROM chip from scratch is a time-consuming and expensive process. For this reason, developers created a type of ROM known as Programmable Read-only Memory (PROM), which can be programmed. If the code or data stored in the PROM has to be changed, the current device must be discarded. As a result, PROM is also known as one-time programmable (OTP) device. Like other ROMs, the information stored in PROM is also non-volatile, but they are more fragile than other ROMs as a jolt of static electricity it can easily cause fuses in the PROM to burn out, changing essential bit pattern from 1 to 0. Nevertheless, blank PROMs are economical and are great for prototyping the data for a ROM before committing to the costly ROM fabrication process. PROM chips are valuable for companies that make their own ROMs from software they write because when they change their code they can create new PROMs without requiring expensive equipment.

Erasable Programmable ROM (EPROM): An EPROM is programmed in exactly the same manner as a PROM. However, unlike PROMs, EPROMs can be erased and reprogrammed repeatedly. An EPROM can be erased by simply exposing the device to a strong source of ultraviolet light for a certain amount of time. Although EPROMs are more expensive than PROMs, their ability to be reprogrammed makes them an essential part of the software development and testing process.

Electrically Erasable Programmable ROM (EEPROM): This type of ROM can be erased by an electrical charge and then written to by using slightly higher-than-normal voltage. EEPROM can be erased one byte at a time, rather than erasing the entire chip with UV light. Hence, the process of re-programming is flexible, but slow. Note that, the chip does not have to be removed for rewrite and neither the entire chip has to be completely erased to change a specific portion of it. In addition, changing the contents does not require additional committed equipment. Because these chips can be changed without opening a casing, they are often used to store programmable instructions in devices, such as printers and other peripherals.

Flash ROM: Flash ROM, also called flash BIOS or flash memory, is a type of constantly powered non-volatile;: memory that can be erased and re-programmed in blocks. It is a variation of EEPROM, which, unlike flash memory, is erased and rewritten at the byte level. Flash memory is often used to hold control code such as the BIOS in a personal computer. When BIOS needs to be ; changed or rewritten, the flash memory can be written in block (rather than byte) sizes, making it easy to update. Flash memory gets its name because the microchip is organized so that a section' of memory cells are erased in a single action or 'flash'. Flash memory is used in digital cellular phones, digital cameras, LAN switches, PC Cards for notebook computers, digital set-up boxes, embedded controllers, and other devices.

Table 4.1 Characteristics of Various ROMs

Type	I Writeable	Erase Size	Cost Per Byte	Speed
Masked ROM	No	N/A	Inexpensive	Fast
PROM	Only once	N/A	Moderate	Fast
EPROM	Yes	Entire chip	Moderate	Fast
EEPROM	Yes	Byte	Expensive	Fast to read slow to erase/write
Flash ROM	Yes	Block	Moderate	Fast to read, slow to erase/write

4.3 Secondary Memory

In the previous sections, we discussed about primary memory, which is volatile in nature and has a very limited storage capacity. This kind of memory is mainly used for processing the data. Being volatile, primary memory cannot hold data or instructions once the computer is switched off. Therefore, a computer requires more stable (non- volatile) type of memory so that it can store all the data (files) and instructions (software programs) even after the computer is turned off. This kind of memory is known as secondary memory or auxiliary memory or peripheral storage or secondary storage. The
secondary storage is used to store data and programs when they are not being processed.

Benefits of Secondary Storage

The benefits of secondary storage can be summarised as follows:

Non-Volatility: By nature, a secondary storage device is non-volatile, that is, it does not lose its contents even when its power is cut ,off.

Capacity: Secondary storage devices are used by organisations so that they can store large volumes of data in.

Reliability: Data in secondary storage is safe because secondary storage is physically reliable.

Convenience: With the help of a computer, authorised people can locate and access data quickly.

Cost: It is less expensive to store data on a tape or disk than to buy and house filing cabinets.

Reusability: The data remains in the secondary storage as long as it is not overwritten or deleted by the user.

Portability: Modern day storage devices like CD-ROMs and floppy disks are so small that they can be easily ported from one computer to another.

Classification of Secondary Storage Devices

Secondary storage devices allow us to store the information and programs permanently. The information in a secondary storage device can be accessed, depending upon how the information is stored on the storage medium. Primarily, there are two methods of accessing data from the secondary storage devices:

Sequential: Sequential access means the computer system must search the storage device from the beginning until it finds the required piece of data. The most common sequential access storage device would be a magnetic tape where data is stored sequentially and can be processed only sequentially.

Direct: Direct access, also known as random access, means that the computer can go directly to the information that the user wants. The most common direct access storage is the disk and the most popular types of disks today are magnetic and optical disks. In this method, information is viewed as a numbered sequence of blocks.

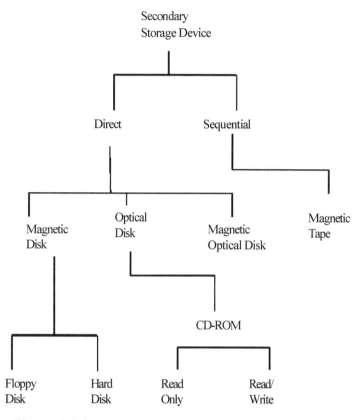

Figure 4.6 Classification of Secondary Storage Devices

4.3.1 Magnetic Tape

Magnetic tape looks like the tape used in music cassettes. It is a plastic tape with magnetic coating. The data is stored in the form of tiny segments of magnetised and de- magnetised portion on the surface of the material. Magnetised portion of the surface refers to the bit value 'l' where as demagnetised portion refers to the bit value '0' . Tapes come in a number of forms, including '1/2-inch wide tape wound on a reel, 1/4-inch wide tape in data cartridges and cassettes, and tapes that look like ordinary music cassettes but are designed to store data instead of music.

The major differences between magnetic tape units are the speed at which the tape is moved past the read/write head and the density of the recorded information. The amount of data or the number of binary digits that can be stored on a linear inch of tape is known as the tape's recording density. Common recording densities for multi-track tapes range from 200 to 6250 bits/bytes per inch (bpi). Note that sometimes the density of a tape is referred to as the number of frames per inch (fpi) or characters per inch (cpi) rather than bpi.

Magnetic Tape Organisation

Magnetic tapes use two reels, supply reel and take-up reel, and the tape moves from the supply reel to the take-up reel (both are mounted on hubs). Figure 4.7 illustrates the basic tape drive mechanism. Note that the tape drive is different for tape reels, cartridges, and cassettes, but all of them work on a similar mechanism.

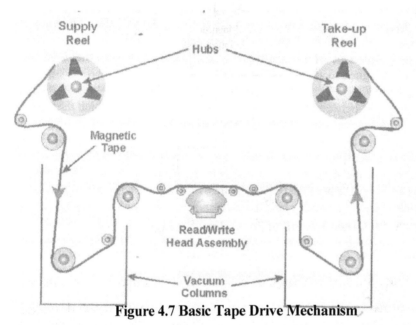

Figure 4.7 Basic Tape Drive Mechanism

The tape is divided into vertical columns (frames) and horizontal rows (channels or tracks). The data is stored in a string of successive columns or frames with one data per frame. Each frame is further divided into rows or tracks. A magnetic tape can typically have 7 to 9 tracks. A bit can be stored in each track, with one byte per frame as shown in Read/Write Figure 4.8. The magnetic tape unit reads and writes Head data in parallel channels or tracks along the length of the tape. Each channel or track is used by a read/ write head (one for each channel), as the tape moves across the magnetic gap of the head. Read/write heads may be either of one gap or of two gaps. The one-gap head has only one magnetic gap at which both reading and writing occur. The two gap head has one gap for reading and another for writing. Although one gap head can be used for reading/writing, the two-gap head gives increased speed by checking while writing. For example, a tape being written on passes over the write gap where the data is recorded, and then the data is read as it passes over the read gap to make a comparison. With this method, errors are detected almost instantly.

A basic unit of data transfer is the byte which is made up of 8-bits. The remaining track (not usually located on the edge of the tape) is a parity track. When a byte is written to the tape, the number of 1 s in the byte is counted, the parity bit is then used to make this number (of Is) even (even parity) or odd (odd parity). Then when the tape is read again, the parity bit is checked to see if any bit has been lost somewhere. In case of odd parity, there must be an odd number of 1 bit represented for each character and even for even parity.

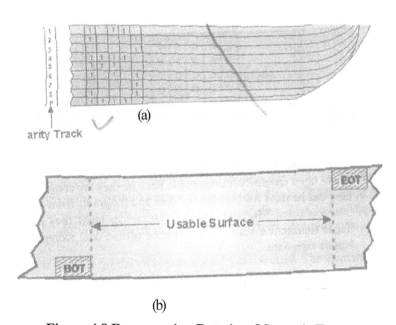

(a)

arity Track

(b)

Figure 4.8 Representing Data in a Magnetic Tape

On a magnetic tape, data is recorded in the forms of blocks, where each block consists of a grouping of data (known as records) that are written or read in a continual manner. Each block can hold one or more records and this process is known as blocking, and the number of records grouped together in each block is known as the blocking factor. Between these blocks, the computer automatically reserves some blank space called inter-block gap (IBG). One block may contain one or more records that are again separated by blank space (usually 0.5 inch) known as inter-record gap (IRG). These gaps allow proper timing for record access figure 4.8(a) and 4.9(b).

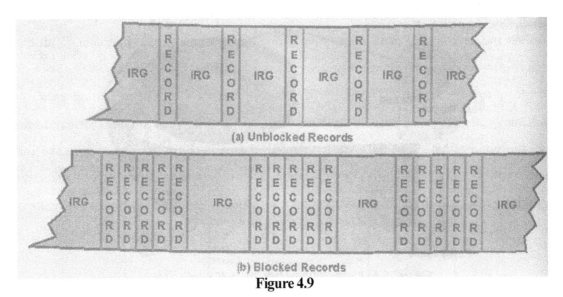

(a) Unblocked Records

(b) Blocked Records

Figure 4.9

Advantages

- Magnetic tapes hold high data recording density, resulting in low cost per bit of storage.

- They have virtually unlimited storage capacity as many tapes and cartridges (as required) can be used to store very large amount of data.

- These tapes are easily transportable because they are compact in size and lightweight.

- Tapes represent a very cheap mode of offline data storage and simple software programs can handle tape data.

Disadvantages of Magnetic Tapes

- Since tapes are sequential access in nature, they are not suitable in situations where data access is required in random order.

- Moreover, data transmission in magnetic tapes is slow as compared to the magnetic disks.

- Magnetic tapes should be kept in a dust free environment as they can cause tape-reading errors.

- High capacity magnetic tape cartridges are more susceptible to damage due to increased linear density, increased track density, and the positioning of the tracks closer to the tape edges.

- Since magnetic tapes use parity bit to check the data, the data on such devices are difficult to recover, even if a minor bit error occurs.
- They are not flexible when file updating requires record insertion and deletion.

4.3.2 Magnetic Disk

Magnetic disks are the most widely used and popular storage medium for direct access secondary storage. They offer high storage capacity, reliability, and have the capability to access the stored data directly. A magnetic disk comprises a thin piece of plastic/metal circular plate/platter, which is coated with magnetic oxide layer. Data is represented as magnetised spots on a disk. A magnetised spot represents a 1(bit) and the absence of a magnetised spot represents a 0 (bit). To read the data, the magnetised data on the disk is converted into electrical impulses, which is transferred to the processor. Writing data onto the disk is accomplished by converting the electrical impulses from the processor into magnetic spots on the disk. The data in a magnetic disk can be erased and reused virtually infinitely. The disk is designed to reside in a protective case or cartridge to shield it from the dust and other external interference.

Storage Organisation of a Magnetic Disk

The surface of a disk is divided into imaginary tracks and sectors. As shown in Figure 4.10, tracks are concentric circles where the data is stored. These tracks are numbered from the outermost ring to the innermost ring, starting with zero from the outermost ring. Disk sectors refer to the number of fixed size areas (imaginary pie slices) that can be accessed by one of the disk drive's read/write heads.

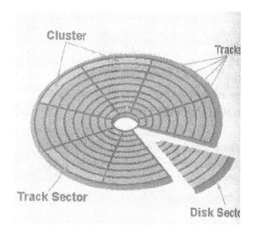

Figure 4.10 Organization of the Disk Surface

59

Generally, a disk has eight or more disk sectors per track. However, different types of magnetic disk may have different number of tracks.

For example, in a 5¼ inch disk, there are 40 tracks with 9 sectors, whereas a 3½ inch disk has 80 tracks with 9 sectors each. Therefore, a 3½-inch disk has twice as many named places on it as a 5¼ inch disk. Modern day disks are marked (tracks and sectors) on both surfaces, hence they are also known as double-sided disks. Each sector is uniquely assigned a disk address before a disk drive can access a piece of data. The disk address comprises sector number, track number, and surface number (if double-sided disks are used). In order to make the disk usable, first it must be formatted to create tracks and sectors.

Multiple disks are maintained and used together to create a large disk storage system. Typically, two, three, or more platters are stacked on top of each (disk pack) other with a common spindle, which turns the whole assembly. There is a gap between the platters, making room for magnetic read/write head. There is a read/write head for each side of each platter, mounted on arms, which can move them towards the central spindle or towards the edge. This concept of stacking the disk is known as cylinder. On a hard disk, a cylinder is made up of all the tracks of the same number from all the metal disks.

Storage Capacity of a Magnetic Disk

There are several parameters, which must be considered in order to find the capacity of a magnetic disk. These parameters include a number of recording surfaces, number of tracks per surface, number of sectors per track, and number of bytes per sector.

Storage capacity of a magnetic disk =

> Number of recording surfaces x
>
> Number of tracks per surface
>
> x Number of sectors per track
>
> x Number of bytes per sector

Accessing Data from a Magnetic Disk

The process of accessing data involves three steps:

Seek time: The time taken by read/write heads are positioned on the specific track number. Typical seek times of modern disks may range between 8 to 12 milliseconds.

Latency time: The time taken by head to wait for the required. The average latency of modern disks ranges from 4.2 to 6.7 ms.

Data transfer rate: The rate at which the data is read from or written to the disk is known as data transfer rate. It is measured in kilobits per second (kbps). Some of the latest hard disks have a data transfer rate of 66 MB per second.

The data transfer rate depends upon the rotational speed of the disk. If the disk has a rotational speed of 6000 rpm (rotations per minute), having 125 sectors and 512 bytes per sector, then the data transfer rate per revolution will be:

125 x 512x6000/60 = 6,4000,00 bytes /second or 6.4 MB/second.

The combined time (seek time, latency, and data transfer time) is known as the access time of the magnetic disk. Specifically, it can be described as the period of time that elapses between a request for information from disk or memory, and the information arriving at the requesting device.

RAM may have an access time of 80 nanoseconds or less, while hard disk access time could be 12-19 milliseconds.

Types of Magnetic Disk

Broadly, magnetic disks can be classified into two types:

- floppy disk
- hard disk

Floppy disk

A floppy disk or diskette is a removable round, flat piece of mylar plastic, coated with ferric oxide and encased in a protective plastic cover (disk jacket). This kind of disk is read and written by a floppy disk drive (FDD). A disk drive is a device that performs the basic operation on a disk, including rotating the disk, reading, and writing data onto the disk. The disk drive's read/write head alters the magnetic orientation of the particles.

Orientation in one-direction represents binary 1 and orientation in the other represents binary 0. Traditionally, floppy disks were used on personal computers to distribute software, transfer data between computers, and create small backups. Before the advent of the hard disk, floppy disks were often used to store a computer's operating system and application software.

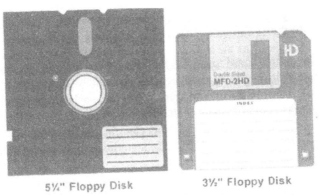

5¼" Floppy Disk   3½" Floppy Disk

Figure 5.12

Various types of Floppy Disks

Diskette Size	Tracks	Number of sectors per side	Capacity per track
5.25 Single Side	40	8	40x8x512=160KB
5.25" Double Side	40	9	2x40x9x512=360KB
5.25" DSHD	80	15	2x80x15x512=1.2MB
3.5" DD	80	9	2x80x9x512=720KB
3.5"HD	80	18	2x80x18x512=1.44MB

Floppy diskettes are small, inexpensive, readily available, and easy to store, and have a good shelf life if stored properly. They also possess the write-protect feature, which allows the users to protect a diskette from being written to. To write-protect a diskette, the user has to press a slide lever towards the edge of the disk, uncovering a hole.

Hard disk

The hard disk, also called the hard drive or fixed disk, is the primary storage unit of the computer. A hard disk consists of a stack of disk platters that are made up of aluminum alloy or glass substrate coated with a magnetic material and protective layers. Many developments have made it possible to store a large amount of data in a small space. The hard drive's speed is discussed in terms of access time (the speed at which the hard drive finds data), which is measured in milliseconds. The average drives have an access time of 9 to 14 ms. The lower the access time, the faster the hard drive.

The speed at which the storage capacity is increased from the day the first hard disk was introduced to modem day hard disks is quite amazing. The capacity, or amount of information that a hard drive can store, is measured in bytes. When IBM introduced the first hard disk in 1956, it could store an amazing (for its time) 5 million characters (about 5 MB). To put that in perspective, the average new computer today comes with a 20-80 GB hard drive. Hard disk plays a significant role in the following important aspects of a computer system:

Performance: The hard disk plays a very important role in overall system performance. The speeds at which the computer boots up and programs load are directly related to the hard disk speed.

Storage Capacity: A bigger hard disk lets one store more software and data into it, thereby permitting the user to store large software related to complex processes such as graphics and multimedia.

Software Support: Nowadays almost all software needs large storage space and faster hard disks to load them efficiently.

Reliability: One way to assess the importance of any hardware component is to consider how much damage is caused in case it fails. By this standard, the hard disk is considered the successful storage component by a long way. Advantages of Magnetic Disks:

- Magnetic disks follow direct access mode for reading and writing onto the data files.
- Magnetic disks are used both as an online and offline storage of data.
- The data transfer rate of disks is much higher than magnetic tapes.

- Due to their low cost and high data recording densities, the cost per bit in magnetic disks is minimum.
- The storage capacity of these disks is virtually unlimited as numbers of such disks can be added to store data.
- Magnetic disks are less prone to the corruption of data as they can withstand the temperature and humidity change in a much better way as compared to magnetic tapes.

Disadvantages of Magnetic Disks

- Magnetic disks must be stored in a dust-free environment in order to protect them from crashing down.
- The cost of magnetic disk storage is more than the cost of magnetic tape.

4.3.3 Optical Disk

An optical is a flat, circular, plastic disk coated with material on which data is stored in the form of highly reflective area and significantly less reflective area. Stored data from optical disk may be read when illuminated with narrow beam source. Optical disks are capable to store high amount of data in limited amount of space.

An optical disk consists long track in the form of spiral shape this track starts from outer edge to the spirals inward to the centre of the disk. This single track makes the optical disk suitable to store large amount of data as shown in figure .

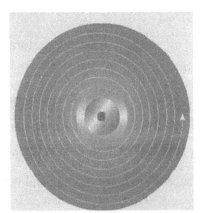

Figure 5.13 Track pattern of optical disk

No doubt it is random access storage device but slower than hard disk, since it is easy to locate storage location.

A compact disk(CD) can store 600-700 MB of information having 12 cm if diameter. Generally, access time of optical disk ranges from 110 to 300 milliseconds.

Types of Optical Disks

Two most widely used optical disks are the

¾ CD-ROM(Compact Disk Read Only Memory)

¾ WORM(Write One Read Many)

CD-ROM Disks

A CD-ROM is a shiny, silver color metal disk of 12 cm in diameter. It is the most is the most popular and least expensive type of optical disk. As the name implies it comes with prerecorded with data, which cannot be altered. A typical optical disk is made of three layers:

* a polycarbonate base- through which light can pass
* a layer of aluminum
* a layer acrylic- proactive layer

Figure 5.14 shows the cross section of CD. Each high area of the CD is called pit, and the flat section is called a land. The pits typically 0.5 microns wide, 0.83 to 3 microns long and 0.15 deep.

Figure 5.14 CD-ROM

A CD-ROM has one track that spirals from the centre to the outside edge. If one could remove the track from a standard 12 cm CD, it would stretch for three and a half miles. The single track is divided into sectors of equal length and density. Files are stored on these particular contiguous sectors. CD-ROM drives are characterised by the rotation speed of the disk and it influences the data access speed.

Since a weak intensity laser is the only thing that touches the surface of the CD directly, there is no wear and tear of disk. However, they can become scratched and unreadable. So in order to protect disks from scratches, strong sunlight, and heat, humidity, and extreme cold, disks should be stored in plastic cases.

WORM (Write Once-Read Many) disks

As the name suggests, WORM (Write Once-Read Many) disks can be used to read as well as to write (usually only once) data onto their surfaces. Data can be written, but cannot be erased on an optical disk. The reason is the technology used for recording: a laser actually burns microscopic pits into the disk's surface. The most common type of a WORM disk is the CD-R (Compact Disk-Recordable). It is a thin (1.2 mm) disk made up of polycarbonate with a 120 mm diameter that is mainly used to store music or data. A CD-R disk is similar to a standard CD, but has differences to enable the storage and removal of data.

A CD-R has usually a storage capacity of 650 MB or 700 MB. A CD-R can be produced by anyone who has a CD-writer (also known as CD-burner), which is a peripheral device that can record data on a CD-R disk, but the data can be recorded only once.

The surface of the CD-ROM contains one long spiral track of data. Along the track, there are flat reflective areas and non-reflective bumps. A flat reflective area represents a binary 1, while a non-reflective bump represents a binary 0. On a new CD-R disk, the entire surface of the disk is reflective; the laser can shine through the dye and reflect off the gold layer. Hence, for a CD-R disk to work there must be a way for a laser to create a non-reflective area on the disk. A CD-R disk therefore has an extra layer that the laser can modify. This extra layer is a greenish dye. When you write data to a CD-R, the writing laser (which is much more powerful than the reading laser) heats up the dye layer and changes its transparency. Therefore, once a section of a CD-R is written, it cannot be erased or rewritten. However, both CD and CD-R drives can read the modified dye as a bump later on.

Advantages of Optical Disks

- Optical disks possess large capacity to store data/information in the form of multimedia, graphics, and video files. They can store more data in less amount of space as compared to magnetic tapes and floppy.

- The life span for data storage in optical disks is considered to be more, about 10-20 years as compared to magnetic disks, which have a comparatively lesser life span.

- Optical disks have low cost per bit of storage as compared to other storage devices.   .

- The magnetic fields do not affect optical disks.

- It is physically harder to break, melt or warp.

- Due to their small size and lightweight, these disks are easily portable and stored.

Disadvantages of Optical Disks

- It is not easy to write data on optical disk.

- They posses slow data access time compared to magnetic disk.

- The optical drive mechanism is complicated as compared to magnetic disk.

****

CHAPTER - 5

Binary Arithmetic

Structure
5.0 Objective
5.1 Introduction
5.2 Binary Addition
5.3 Binary Subtraction
5.4 Binary Multiplication
5.5 Binary Division

5.0 Objective: Objective of this lesson is to specify the rules to perform four principle arithmetic operations- addition, subtraction, multiplication, division of binary numbers with the help of suitable examples. Further, it is to define two types of real numbers viz. fixed point representation, floating point representation; within floating point(non-normalized and normalized) and their representations in computer memory are also discussed. Rules to perform arithmetic operations(Addition, Subtraction, Multiplication, Division) with normalized floating numbers are also listed out. At the end the various types of errors with measurement that can be introduced during numerical computation are also defined.

5.1 Introduction

Binary arithmetic is essential for performing arithmetic operation in computer systems. To understand what is going on in the computer's arithmetic logic unit(ALU), the basics of binary addition, subtraction, multiplication , and division operations must be understood. These operations can only be understood if we get familiar with the storage of number in computer memory.

5.2 Binary Addition

Binary addition is exactly same as decimal addition, except the rules. The binary addition rules are shown in Table 5.1

Table 5.1

A(Augend)	B(Addend)	A+B(SUM)	Carry
0	0	0	0
0	1	1	0
1	0	1	01
1	1	0	

Example 5.1 Add $(110101)_2$ with $(101110)_2$

      Carry

      Augend   010011   (+19)

      Addend 101100 (+44)

     Sum   111111 (+63)

Example 5.2 Add $(0111)_2$ with $(0011)_2$

Carry 111

Augend 0111 (+7)

Addend 0011 (+3)

Sum   1010 (+10)

5.3 Binary Subtraction
5.3.1 Unsigned Numbers

Likewise in the decimal system we subtract decimal digit from a smaller digit by borrowing from next column, the same rule can be adopted in binary subtraction also. The rules for binary subtraction are shown in Table 5.2

Table 5.2

A (Minuend)	B (Subtrahend)	A-B (Difference)	Borrow
0	0	0	00
	1	1	11
	0	1	01
	1	0	0

Example 5.3

     Subtract $(1001)_2$ from $(101111)_2$

          Borrow

          Minuend   101111 (+47)

          Subtrahend   1001 (+09)

          Difference   100110 (+38)

Example 5.4

Subtract $(011)_2$ from $(101)_2$

Borrow	1
Minuend	101 (+5) 011
Subtrahend	(+3)

Difference	010 (+2)

5.3.2 Signed Numbers

The method which has been described till now for binary subtraction is not well suited for the computer. If this method is adopted we must have separate algorithm for subtraction. As you know that subtraction of **b** from **a** means addition of (**-b**) to **a**.

In computer, binary subtraction is transferred into addition by using:

a. One's complement method. **b.**

Two's complement method.

The advantage is that we could use a single algorithm to implement addition as well as subtraction. In general there are (radix-1)'s complement and radix's complement. 1's and 2's complement of positive numbers is identical to sign magnitude.

Methods to represent negative numbers

The three widely used methods to represent negative numbers:

a. Signed bit magnitude representation

b. 1's complement representation **c.** 2's

complement representation

70

5.4 Binary multiplication 5.4.1 Unsigned Numbers

Binary multiplication can be accomplished using the same method that is used for multiplication of decimal numbers. Rules for binary multiplication:

Table 3.3

A	B	AxB
0	0	0
0	1	0
1	0	0
1	1	1

Product of two 'n' bit numbers will require upto '2n' bits to accommodate the result.

Example 5.10

```
        (+5) 101 (Multiplicand)
        (+6) 110 (Multiplier)
          --- 000
          101 101
          ---------
      (+30) 11110 (Product)
          ---------
```

****

CHAPTER - 6
Computer Languages

Structure

6.0 Objective

6.1 Introduction

6.2 Generations of Programming Languages

6.3 Programming Paradigm

6.4 Translators

6.5 Linker

6.6 Loader

6.0 Objective

The objective of this lesson is to discuss the prominent concepts related to natural languages and computer languages. Further this lesson acquaints the users the different generations of programming languages with their advantages and disadvantages. The various programming paradigm are also discussed in this lesson, means the way in which a program is written in order to solve a problem. The various programming languages used to communicate with computer are listed out. The lesson also elaborates the stages required during translation process(HLL, Assembly language to machine code).

6.1 Introduction

A language is a system of communications. It usually consists of all the verbal or written symbols and expressions that are used to exchange ideas and information. Communication can take place between individuals or between an individual and a machine such as a computer.

Why we need programming languages?

Computer programs are instructions to the computer. You tell a computer what to do through programs. Without programs, a computer is an empty machine. Computers do not understand human languages, so you need to use computer languages to communicate with them.

Programming language consists of set of characters, symbols, and usage rules that allow the users to communicate with computers, like wise natural language. The main reason behind it that natural languages(English, Hindi) are poor structured, ambiguous, and has very large vocabularies.

On the other side, computer languages have exactly defined rules, strictly controlled vocabularies. In case of natural languages, we can understand even while using poor grammar and vocabulary. However, in case of programming language, the rules are very rigid, thus the programmer has to follow all the specified rules. The language a computer speaks is the computer's native language or machine language.

6.2 Generation of Programming Languages

Since 1940's programming languages have evolved. With each passing years, the languages become user-friendly and more powerful. This resulted into the development of hundred of languages. We can categories development of all languages in five generations.

6.2.1 First Generation (Machine Language): 1940-1950

This is the lowest form of computer language. When the first generation computers were introduced, programs were written only in binary based machine level language. This the only language actually understood by computer.

Computers are digital devices, which have only two states, **ON** and **OFF**(1 and 0). Hence, computers can understand only binary code. Therefore every instruction and data should be written using **0's** and **1's**.

The **machine language** is a set of primitive instructions built into every computer. The instructions are in the form of binary code, so you have to enter binary codes for various instructions. In other words, the binary language(the language of 0's and 1's) is the machine language. Any instruction in machine language is known as machine instruction.

For example:

0101 0100 1010 0110

could represent a 16 bit machine instruction.

Programming with native machine language is a tedious process. Moreover the programs are highly difficult to read and modify. An instruction prepared in machine language will have at least two parts. The first part is the command or operation, and it tells the computer what function to be performed. The second part represents the address where data is stored to be operated.

a) Operation code(Op code)

b) Address or Addresses of one or more memory location containing an operand or operands or address of another instruction.

Disadvantages:

- **Complex Language**: The programmer has to remember the code number for Op code, and the addresses of all the data items, it is very difficult task.

- **Machine Dependent**: Machine language is machine dependent.

- Error-Prone: It requires a super human effort to keep track of the logic of the problem and, therefore results in frequent programming errors.

- **Tedious**: Any modification in machine language results in series of changes, in other words modification in machine language is difficult task.

Advantages:

No doubt writing and modification of machine language is tedious and difficult job but this language has certain advantages, as follows:

- **High Speed**: Program written in machine language takes shorter time in execution.

- **Translator Free**: No translator(compiler or interpreter) is required.

6.2.2 Second Generation (Assembly language): 1950-1958

Assembly language is a also low-level programming language in which a mnemonic is used to represent each of the machine language instructions.

To reduce the programmer's burden, symbolic languages (which are sometimes called assembly language) were developed in 1950's main developer was IBM. However, Jack Powell, Bob Navelen, Clement and Michael Bradely also helped in the development of the assembly language. This language was introduced for second generation computers. This permits the use of alphanumeric symbols (numbers and letters) instead of numeric operation codes, memory addresses, and data. These symbols are mnemonic, which are two to three abbreviations for the functions performed by the instructions. Assembly languages were developed to make programming easy.

General format of assembly instruction is:

[Label] <opcode> <operands> [; Comment]

If multiple operands are used, each of them separated by comma. Comments are optional; they are to included to facilitate proper documentation. For example,

Label	Opcode	Operands	Comments
BEGIN	ADD	A, B	; Add B to A

Since the computer cannot understand assembly language, however, a program called assembler is used to convert assembly language program into machine code, as shown in Figure 6.2. Once the assembly language source program is converted into machine code, the assembler is no long 75 ded. Assembler translates a source program to an object program on a one-to-one basis. That is, one assembly language mnemonic translates into one machine code instruction.

This language is called low-level language because it is designed for particular machine. It cannot be developed without knowing the size of the memory and size of location word.

Since assembly language is machine-dependent, an assembly program can only be executed on a particular machine. Assembly programs are written in terms of mnemonic names easy-to-remember than machine instructions written in terms of 0's and 1's. Each processor family has its own assembly language.

Advantages

- **Easier to Maintain**: Assembly languages are easy to modify.
- **Less Error-Prone**: Less error is made, if introduced easier to find.
- **Easy to Understand and Use**: Operation codes in machine language are replaced by mnemonics, and memory addresses in machine languages are replaced by variable names which are easier to remember.

Disadvantages

- **Machine Dependent**: These languages are machine dependent.
- **Less Efficient**: A program written in assembly language takes more execution time compared to machine language.
- **Translator Required**: An extra program assembler is required for assembly language to convert onto machine language.

6.2.3 Third Generation (High-level Language) 1958-85

During 1960's , computers started to gain popularity and it became necessary to develop languages that were more like natural languages such as English so that a common user could use the computer efficiently.

High-level language instructions closely resemble with human language and mathematical notation. These languages are easy to learn and programs may be written in these languages with much less effort. These languages do not require that programmer to have detailed knowledge of internal working of the computer. These languages are independent of the structure of the specification of computer, so a program written in such language can be used in different machines.

The high-level languages were developed in order to overcome the platform specific problem and make programming easier. The high-level languages are English-like and easy to learn. There are over one hundred high-level languages.

The popular languages used today are:

¾ COBOL (COmmon Business Oriented Language)

¾ FORTRAN (FORmula TRANslation)

¾ BASIC (Beginner's All-purpose Symbolic Instructional Code)

¾ Pascal (named for Blaise Pascal)

¾ Ada (named for Augusta Ada Lovelace the first lady programmer)

¾ C (whose developer designed B first)

¾ Visual Basic (Basic-like visual language developed by Microsoft)

¾ Delphi (Pascal-like visual language developed by Borland)

¾ C++ (an object-oriented language, based on C)

Each of these languages was designed for a specific purpose. COBOL was designed for business applications and now is used primarily for business data processing. FORTRAN was designed for mathematical computations and is used mainly for numeric computations. BASIC, as its name suggests, was designed to be learned and used easily. Ada was developed for the Department of Defense and is mainly used in defense projects. C combines the power of an assembly language with the ease of use and portability of a high-level language. Visual Basic and Delphi are used in developing graphical user interfaces and in rapid application development. C++ is popular for system software projects like writing compilers and operating systems. Microsoft Windows 95 was coded using C++.

A program written in a high-level language is called a **source program**. Since a computer cannot understand source program, a program called a compiler or interpreter is used to translate the source program into a machine language program called an **object program.** The object program is often then linked with other supporting library code before the object can be executed on the machine.

You can run a source program on any machine with appropriate compilers. The source program must be recompiled, however, because the object program can only run on a specific machine.

Following BASIC code will calculate the sum of two numbers:

```
LET X=20
LET Y=10
LET SUM = X+Y
PRINT SUM
STOP
END
```

Now-a-days computers are networked to work together. Java was designed to run object programs on any platform. With Java, you write the program once and compile the source program into a special type of object code. The object code can then run on any machine that can interpret it.

Advantages

- **Easy to Learn**: These are easier to learn than assembly language. These require less time to write. These have extensive vocabulary, symbols and sentences.

- **Easier to Maintain**: As compared to LLL these languages are easier to maintain.

- **Machine Independent**: These languages are machine independent.

- **Built-in Functions**: Libraries of subroutines are incorporated and used in many other programs.

- **Easy Documentation**: They provide better documentation.

- **Low Development Cost**: More than one low-level language instructions are reduced to single high-level language instruction.

- **Readability**: The writing of source code in HLL does not require the knowledge of the internal working of the computer.

Disadvantages

Less Efficient: The HLL are less efficient as far as computation time is concerned.

Poor Control on Hardware: Programmers do not have to know the internal architecture of computer. As a result program written in HLL cannot completely use the internal structure.   78

6.2.4 Fourth-Generation Language(4GLs) :1985 onwards

Fourth generation languages are simply English like syntax rules, commonly used to access databases. These languages are non-procedural languages. The non-procedural method is simply to state the needed output instead of specifying each step one after the other to perform a task. In other words, the computer is instructed what it must do rather than how a computer must perform a task.

4GLs have minimum number of syntax rules. Hence, common people can also use such languages to write application programs. This saves time and allows professional programmers to solve more complex tasks. The 4GLs are divided into three categories:

- **Query Languages**: They allow the user to retrieve information from databases by following simple syntax rules.

- **Repot Generators**: They produce costomised report using data stored in database.

- **Application Generator**: With application generators, the user writes programs to allow data to be entered into database.

4GLs are designed to be user friendly and interactive, and to help you quickly develop an application package. In general such products are marked by:

- Non-procedural programming code;
- A simple query language;
- Centered around database.

6.2.5 Fifth Generation Language: Very High-Level Language

These languages will have capability to process natural language. The computer will be able to accept, interpret, and execute instructions in a native or natural language of the end-users. The users will be free from learning any programming language to communicate with the computers. The Programmers simply type the instructions or tell the computer by the way of microphones what it needs to do. These languages are closely linked to artificial intelligence and expert systems.

***

CHAPTER – 7
Operating System

Structure

7.0 Objective

7.1 Introduction

7.2 Functions of Operating System

7.3 Components of Operating System

7.4 Types of Operating System

7.0 Objective

This lesson provides an outlook on the basic role of operating

system in modern day computers; learn about the general functions and components of

operating system; know about the different

types of operating systems; providing an overview of UNIX operating system.

7.1 Introduction

In the early days computers were interacted with hardware through machine language. A software was required which could perform basic tasks, such as recognizing input form the keyboard, sending output to the display devices., keeping track of files and directories on the disk. In order to control all such activities software was introduced for modern computers, called an operating system

(OS). This software is put at the top of memory.

Software is general term that is used to describe any single

program or group of programs. Software used by a computer can be broadly classified into three categories.

In this lesson we will discuss a special type of a system software, termed as OS that controls all the computer resources and provides the base upon which the applications and utilities can be developed and run.

On today's computers, application programs cannot run without an operating system. The inter relationship of hardware, operating system, application software, and user is shown in Figure 7.2.

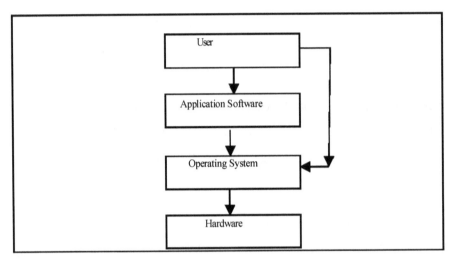

Figure 7.2 Inter relationship of hardware, operating system, application software, and user

Definition

An operating system is an integrated set of programs that controls the recourses (the CPU, memory, I/O devices etc.) of a computer system and acts as an interface or virtual machine that is more convenient to use than bare machine. Figure 7.3 shows logical architecture of a computer system.

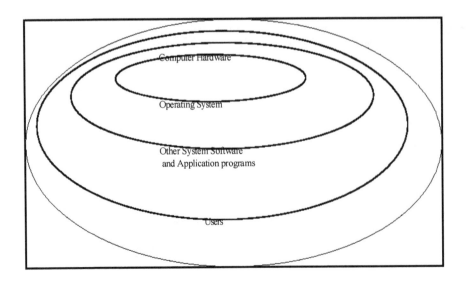

Figure 7.3 Logical architecture of Computer System

It acts as an intermediary between a user and the computer hardware.

The operating system is a piece of software that manages and controls a computer's activities

Why we need OS?

An operating system is the most important program in a computer system. It is the interface between application program and the computer hardware.

The two main features of the Operating System are:

- Convince to the user.

- Effective utilization of hardware devices.

An operating system can be viewed as resource allocator. A computer system has many resources (hardware and software) that may be required to solve a problem(CPU time, memory space, file storage space, I/O devices etc.).

The major tasks of the operating systems are:
- Allocating and assigning system resources.
- Scheduling operations.
- Monitoring system activities.

Allocating and Assigning System Resources

The OS is responsible for determining what computer resources (CPU, memory, disks, input and output devices) a program needs and for allocating and assigning them to run the program.

Scheduling Operations

The OS is responsible for scheduling programs to use the system resources efficiently.

Monitoring system activities

Many of today's operating systems support such techniques as multiprogramming, multithreading, or multiprocessing to increase system performance.

Multiprogramming allows multiple programs to run simultaneously through sharing of the CPU. The CPU is much faster than the other components. As a result, it is idle most of the time; for example, while waiting for data to be transferred from the disk or from other sources. A multiprogramming OS takes advantage of this by allowing multiple programs to use the CPU when it would otherwise be idle. For example, you may use a word processor to edit a file while the web browser is downloading a file at the same time.

Multithreading allows concurrency within a program, so that its subunits can run at the same time. For example, a word-processing program allows users to edit text and save it to a file at the same time. In this example, editing and saving are two tasks within the same application.

Multiprocessing, or parallel processing, uses two or more processors together to perform task. It is like a surgical operation where several doctors work together on one patient.

As the manager of these resources, the operating system allocates them to specific programs and users as necessary for their tasks.

5.2 Functions of Operating System

The main functions performed by most OS are as follows:

Process Management

Processing jobs deciding on the job scheduling technique and how long a job is to be processed, releasing the processor when the jobs are terminated.

Memory Management

As a memory manager, the OS handles the allocation and dead location of memory space as required by various programs.

Device Management

OS provides I/O subsystem between process and device driver. It also detects device failures and notifies the same to the user.

File Management

OS is responsible to creation, deletion of files and directories. It also takes care of other file related activates such as retrieving, naming, and protecting the files.

Security Management

OS protects system resources and information against destruction and from unauthorized use.

Command Interpretation

The command interpretation is the layer that actually interacts with the

computer operator. It consists of set of commands through which user communicate the program.

In addition to the above listed major functions, an operating system also performs few other functions such as keeping an account of which users use what kind of computer recourses and how much etc. The common functions of controlling and allocating resources are then brought

together into one piece of software- is called an the operating system.

7.3 Components of an Operating System

There are two main components of operating system:

- Command Interpreter
- Kernel

7.3 Types of Operating System

Modern computer operating systems may be classified into three categories according to the nature of interaction that takes place between the user and user's program during its processing. The three categories are - batch process, time-shared, real-time operating system.

7.3.1 Single User - Single Processing System

The simplest of all the computer systems is a single use-single processor system. It has a single processor, runs a single program and interacts with a single user at a time. The operating system for this system is very simple to design and implement. However, the CPU is not utilized to its full potential, because it sits idle for most of the time.

Figure 7.5 Single user - single processor system

In this configuration, all the computing resources are available to the user all the time. Therefore, operating system has very simple responsibility. A representative example of this category of operating system is MS-DOS.

7.3.2 Batch Processing Operating System

In batch processing operating system environment users submit jobs to a central place where these jobs are collected in batch, and subsequently placed in an input queue in the computer where they are run. In this case, user has no interaction with the job during its processing, and computer response time is turnaround time, that is, the time from submission of the job until execution is complete and results are ready for return to the person who submits the job.

The main function of a batch processing system is to automatically keep executing one job to the next job in the batch(Figure 7.4). The main idea behind a batch processing system is to reduce the interference of the operator during the processing or execution of jobs by the computer. All functions of a batch processing system are carried out by the batch monitor. The batch monitor permanently resides in the low end of the main store. The current jobs out of the whole batch are executed in the remaining storage area. In other words, a batch monitor is responsible for controlling all the environment of the system operation. The batch monitor accepts batch initiation commands from the operator, processes a job, and performs the job of job termination and batch termination.

In a batch processing system, we generally make use of the term 'turn around time'. It is defined as the time from which a user job is given to the time when its output is given back to the user. This time includes the batch formation time, time taken to execute a batch, time taken to print results and the time required to physically sort the printed outputs that belong to different jobs. As the printing and sorting of the results is done for all the jobs of batch together, the turn around time for a job becomes the function of the execution time requirement of all jobs in the batch. You can reduce the turn around time for different jobs by recording the jobs or faster input output media like magnetic tape or disk surfaces. It takes very less time to read a record from these media. For instance, it takes round about five milliseconds for a magnetic 'tape' and about one millisecond for a fast fixed-head disk in comparison to a card reader or printer that takes around 50-100 milliseconds. Thus, if you use a disk or tape, it reduces the amount of time the central processor has to wait for an input output operation to finish before resuming processing. This would reduce the time taken to process a job which indirectly would bring down the turn-around times for all the jobs in the batch.

Another term that is commonly used in a batch processing system is Job Scheduling. Job scheduling is the process of sequencing jobs so that they can be executed on the processor. It recognizes different jobs on the basis of first-come-first-served (FCFS) basis. It is because of the sequential nature of the batch. The batch monitor always starts the next job in the batch. However, in exceptional cases, you could also arrange the different jobs in the batch depending upon the priority of each batch. Sequencing of jobs according to some criteria requires scheduling the jobs at the time of creating or executing a batch. On the basis of relative importance of jobs, certain 'priorities' could be set for each batch of jobs. Several batches could be formed on the same criteria of priorities. So, the batch having the highest priority could be made to run earlier than other batches. This would give a better turn around service to the selected jobs.

7.3.3 Multiprogramming Operating System

Multiprogramming operating system is a system that allows more than one active user program (or part of user program) to be stored in the main memory simultaneously. Having several programs in memory at the same time requires some form of memory management. In addition, if several jobs are ready to run at the same time system must choose the order in which each job has to be selected and executed one after the other. This decision is CPU scheduling. Finally multiple jobs runs concurrently require that their ability to affect one another be limited in all phases of the operating system, including process scheduling, disk storage, and memory management.

The objective of a multiprogramming operating system is to increase the system utilization efficiency. The batch processing system tries to reduce the CPU idle time through operator interaction. However, it cannot reduce the idle time due to IO operations. So, when some IO is being performed by the currently executing job of a batch, the CPU sits idle without any work to do. Thus, the multiprogramming operating system tries to eliminate such idle times by providing multiple computational tasks for the CPU to perform. This is achieved by keeping multiple jobs in the main store. So, when the job that is being currently executed on the CPU needs some I/O, the CPU passes its requirement over to the I/O processor. Till the time the I/O operation is being carried out, the CPU is free to carry out some other job. The presence of independent jobs guarantees that the CPU and I/O activities are totally independent of each other. However, if it was not so, then it could lead to some erroneous situations leading to some time- dependent errors.

Some of the most popular multiprogramming operating systems are:

UNIX, VMS, Window NT etc.

Different forms of multiprogramming operating systems involve multitasking, multiprocessing, muti-user operating system.

7.3.4 Multitasking Operating System

Multitasking means the ability to load more than one program at time. With this facility we can do two or more than two jobs simultaneously. For example one job is printed out and other job on the screen. You may take a printout from a database package while typing a letter on the screen. Multitasking can take place either at single-user(one screen more than one programs) or multi- user (different screens more than one programs). Note that multiprogramming implies multitasking, but multitasking does not imply multiprogramming. Multitasking means one of the mechanisms that the multiprogramming operating system employs in managing the totality of computer-related resources such as CPU, memory, and I/O devices.

Examples: UNIX, WINDOWS 2000/XP

7.3.5 Multi-user Operating System
It allows simultaneous access to a computer system through one or more terminals.

Note multi-user operating system does not imply multiprogramming or multitasking.

Time sharing systems incorporate the features of multi-user and multiprogramming

7.3.6 Multiprocessing System
So far we have considered systems with a single CPU. However,

we have seen that use I/O processor can be improved by making possible concurrent use of more than one task. It is a computer hardware configuration that includes more than one independent processing unit. Performance of I/O processor can further be improved by designing more than one CPU. Such systems are called multiprocessing systems and operating system for such a system so desire is called multiprocessing OS. The multiprogramming is used to describe interconnected computer configuration, or computers with two or more CPUs which have the ability to simultaneously execute several programs. In such a system instructions from different and independent programs can be processed simultaneously by different CPUs or the CPUs may simultaneously execute different instructions from the same program.

Figure 7.8 Basic organization of multiprocessing

Multiprocessing systems can be:

- tightly coupled: there is single system wide memory which is shared by all processors.

-loosely coupled: processors do not share memory, each processor has its own local memory.

Note multiprocessing systems are multitasking systems by definition because they support simultaneous execution of multiple processes on different processor.

Examples : LINUX, UNIX, WINDOW 2002/XP.

7.3.9 Network Operating System

A networked operating system is a collection of physically interconnected computers.

A network operating system is a collection of software and associated protocol that allow a set of autonomous computers interconnected computer network to be used together in a convenient and cost-effective manner.

Characteristics of network operating system:

- Each computer has its own private operating system instead of running as part of a global system-wide operating system.

- Users are typically of where each of their files are kept and must move a file from one system to another.

Table 7.1 is a brief summary of various operating systems.

Table 7.1

Batch processing	Automatically keep executing one job to the next job in the batch
Multiprogramming	Single CPU divides time between more than one jobs.
Multiprocessing	Multiple CPUs perform more than one job at a time.
Multitasking	It is described as any system that runs or appears to run more than application program at any given time.
Time Sharing	It is special case of multiprogramming where a single CPU serves a number of users at interactive terminals.

7.4 An Overview of UNIX Operating System

UNIX is a multi-user, multitasking, time sharing operating system. It was developed in 1969 at Bell Laboratories by Ken Thompson and Dennis Ritchie. It was the first operating system to be written in C language. That is, why it becomes easy to move it to a new machine-portability. This was important reason for its large popularity and availability on a wide variety of systems.

Characteristics of UNIX

- Portability
- Open system
- Rich and productive programming environment
- Communication
- Multi-user capability
- Multitasking

Components of UNIX

UNIX has major three components:

¾ Kernel
¾ Command Interpreter
¾ File System

Figure 7.9 shows the architecture of UNIX.

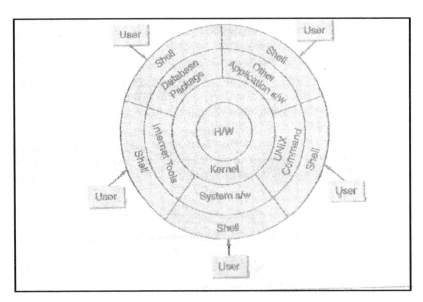

Figure 7.9 shows the architecture of UNIX

Kernel

It is known as the base operating system. It controls the computer resources. When the user logs on, the kernel runs **init** and **getty** to check if the user is authorized has the correct password. Kernel provides the following functions:

- Process scheduling
- Memory management
- Device management
- File management
- System call interface
- Process synchronization and inter-process communication
- Operator console interface

The utility programs and UNIX commands are not considered as part of UNIX kernel. Kernel consists of layers closest to the hardware that are the for the most part protected from the user. Kernel communicates directly with hardware. The kernel does not deal directly with a user.

Some Popular Operating Systems

MSDOS, Windows 95, Windows 2000, Windows NT, Windows XP, OS/2, LINUX, UNIX, VMS, NetWare.

****

94

CHAPTER - 8
Computer Generations

Structure

8.0 Objective

8.1 Introduction

8.1.1 First Generation Computers

8.1.2. Second Generation Computers

8.1.3. Third Generation Computers

8.1.4. Fourth Generation Computers

8.1.5. Fifth Generation Computers

8.0 Objective

After reading this lesson you will be able to understand the evolution of computers, from refining of abacus to supercomputers; the advancement in technology that has changed the way computers operate, efficient, size, and cost.

8.1 Introduction

In computer terminology, the word **'generation'** is described as a stage of technological development or innovation. A computer belongs to a generation is determined by the technology it uses. A major technological development that fundamentally changed the way computers operate, resulting in increasingly smaller, cheaper, more powerful, and more efficient and reliable devices introduced in each generation of computer. According to kind of processors installed, superior operating systems and other software utilities there are five generations of computers. Figure 1.1 illustrates the first three generations of computers that incorporate drastic changed in computer technology.

Figure 8.1 First Three generations of computers

8.1.1 First Generation Computers (1937-1953) : Vacuum Tubes

First Generation computers are characterized by the use of vacuum tubes/thermionic valves. These vacuum tubes were used for calculation as well as storage and control. Later, magnetic tapes and magnetic drums were implemented as storage media.

The first general purposes programmable electronic computer was the Electronic Numerical Integrator and Computer (ENIAC), built by J. Presper Eckert and John V. Mauchly at the University of Pennsylvania. Work began in 1943, funded by the Army Ordnance Department, which needed a way to compute ballistics during World War II. The machine wasn't completed until 1945, but then it was used extensively for calculations during the design of the hydrogen bomb. By the time it was decommissioned in 1955 it had been used for research on the design of wind tunnels, random number generators, and weather prediction. The first vacuum tube computer, ENIAC, had about 17,000 vacuum tubes and 7000 resisters. The machine weighed 30 tons, covered about 1000 square feet of floor, and consumed 130 or 140 kilowatts of electricity. The ENIAC's clock speed was about 100 kHz. In addition to ballistics, the ENIAC's field of application included weather prediction, atomic-energy calculations, cosmic-ray studies, thermal ignition, random-number studies, wind-tunnel design, and other scientific uses. No electronic computers were being applied to commercial problems until about 1951.

Eckert, Mauchly, and John von Neumann, a consultant to the ENIAC project, began work on a new machine before ENIAC was finished. "Von Neumann designed the Electronic Discrete Variable Automatic Computer (EDVAC) in 1945 with a memory to hold both a stored program as well as data." Von Neumann's computer allowed for all the computer functions to be controlled by a single source. The main contribution of EDVAC, their new project, was the notion of a stored program. There is some controversy over who deserves the credit for this idea, but none over how important the idea was to the future of general purpose computers. ENIAC was controlled by a set of external switches and dials; to change the program required physically altering the settings on these controls. These controls also limited the speed of the internal electronic operations. Through the use of a memory that was large enough to hold both instructions and data, and using the program stored in memory to control the order of arithmetic operations, EDVAC was able to run orders of magnitude faster than ENIAC. By storing instructions in the same medium as data, designers could concentrate on improving the internal structure of the machine without worrying about matching it to the speed of an external control.

Then in 1951 came the Universal Automatic Computer (UNIVAC I), designed by Remington rand and collectively owned by US census bureau and General Electric. UNIVAC amazingly predicted the winner of 1952, presidential elections, Dwight D. Eisenhower. Eckert and Mauchly later developed what was arguably the first commercially successful computer, the UNIVAC; in 1952, 45 minutes after the polls closed and with 7% of the vote counted, UNIVAC predicted Eisenhower would defeat Stevenson with 438 electoral votes (he ended up with 442).

In first generation computers, the operating instructions or programs were specifically built for the task for which computer was manufactured. The Machine language was the only way to tell these machines to perform the operations. There was great difficulty to program these computers, and more when there were some malfunctions.

Examples: ENIAC, EDVAC, UNIVAC

Characteristics of first generation computers

- These computer are based on the vacuum tube technology.
- These computers were very large, require lot of space for installation.
- Since thousands of vacuum tubs were used, they generated a large amount of heat.
- They are slow and lacked in versatility.
- They required large amount of electricity.

- These machines are prone to frequent hardware failures therefore maintenance cost is very large.

- Since machine languages are used these computers are difficult to program and use.

8.1.2 Second Generation (1954-1962): Transistors

The second generation saw several important developments at all levels of computer system design, from the technology used to build the basic circuits to the programming languages used to write scientific applications.

Electronic switches in this era were based on discrete diode and transistor technology with a switching time of approximately 0.3 microseconds. The first machines to be built with this technology include TRADIC at Bell Laboratories in 1954 and TX-0 at MIT's Lincoln Laboratory. Memory technology was based on magnetic cores which could be accessed in random order, as opposed to mercury delay lines, in which data was stored as an acoustic wave that passed sequentially through the medium and could be accessed only when the data moved by the I/O interface, important innovations in computer architecture included index registers for controlling loops and floating point units for calculations based on real numbers. Prior to this accessing successive elements in an array was quite tedious and often involved writing self-modifying code (programs which modified themselves as they ran; at the time viewed as a powerful application of the principle that programs and data were fundamentally the same, this practice is now frowned upon as extremely hard to debug and is impossible in most high level languages). Floating point operations were performed by libraries of software routines in early computers, but were done in hardware in second generation machines.

During this second generation many high level programming languages were introduced, including FORTRAN (1956), ALGOL (1958), and COBOL (1959). Important commercial machines of this era include the IBM 704 and its successors, the 709 and 7094. The latter introduced I/O processors for better throughput between I/O devices and main memory.

100

The second generation also saw the first two supercomputers designedspecifically for numeric processing in scientific applications. The term ``supercomputer'' is generally reserved for a machine that is an order of magnitude more powerful than other machines of its era. Two machines of the 1950s deserve this title. The Livermore Atomic Research Computer (LARC) and the IBM 7030 (aka Stretch) were early examples of machines that overlapped memory operations with processor operations and had primitive forms of parallel processing.

The transistor (G) characterized the second-generation computers. Transistors were made of a semiconducting material and controlled the flow of electricity through the circuits. They also allowed computers to become smaller and more powerful and faster at the same time. The transistor was invented in 1947, won the Nobel Prize in 1956 but was not used in computers until 1959. They were also less expensive, smaller, required less electricity, and emitted less heat than vacuum tubes.

Magnetic tape was still the most commonly used external storage medium, while magnetic disk storage was used so data could be located more rapidly. MIT developed magnetic core storage in which each core stored one bit of information. Punched cards and magnetic tape were still used for input, while punched cards and paper constituted the output.

Programming languages became more sophisticated as high-level languages (such as FORTRAN, COBOL, BASIC, and PL/I) resembling English were developed. however, computers were still under the control of human operators.

Examples: PDP-8, IBM1400 series, IBM 7090, Honywell 400,800 series

Characteristics of second generation computers

- These machines are based upon transistors technology.

101

- They are smaller as compared to first generation computers.

- Computational time reduced from milliseconds to microseconds.

- They are more reliable and less prone to hardware failure.

- These had better portability and generated less amount of heat.

- Assembly language was used to program computers. Hence, programming became more

- time-efficient and less cumbersome.

- Still required air conditioning.

8.4.3 Third Generation (1963-1972) : Integrated Circuits

The third generation brought huge gains in computational power. Innovations in this era include the use of integrated circuits, or ICs (semiconductor devices with several transistors built into one physical component), semiconductor memories starting to be used instead of magnetic cores, microprogramming as a technique for efficiently designing complex processors, the coming of age of pipelining and other forms of parallel processing ,the introduction of operating systems and time- sharing.

The first ICs were based on small-scale integration (SSI) circuits, which had around 10 devices per circuit (or ``chip''), and evolved to the use of medium-scale integrated (MSI) circuits, which had up to 100 devices per chip. Multilayered printed circuits were developed and core memory was replaced by faster, solid state memories. Computer designers began to take advantage of parallelism by using multiple functional units, overlapping CPU and I/O operations, and pipelining (internal parallelism) in both the instruction stream and the data stream. In 1964, Seymour Cray developed the CDC 6600, which was the first architecture to use functional parallelism. By using 10 separate functional units that could operate simultaneously and 32 independent memory banks, the CDC 6600 was able to attain a computation rate of 1 million floating point operations per second (1 Mflops). Five years later CDC released the 7600, also developed by SeymourCray. The CDC 7600, with its pipelined functional units, is considered to be thefirst vector processor and was capable of executing at 10 Mflops. The IBM 360/91, released during the same period, was roughly twice as fast as the CDC 660. It employed instruction look ahead, separate floating point and integer functional units and pipelined instruction stream. The IBM 360-195 was comparable to the CDC 7600, deriving much of its performance from a very fast cache memory. The SOLOMON computer, developed by Westinghouse Corporation, and the ILLIAC IV, jointly developed by Burroughs, the Department of Defense and the University of Illinois, were representative of the first parallel computers. The Texas Instrument Advanced Scientific Computer (TI-ASC) and the STAR-100 of CDC were pipelined vector processors that demonstrated the viability of that design and set the standards for subsequent vector processors.

Early in this third generation Cambridge and the University of London cooperated in the development of CPL (Combined Programming Language, 1963). CPL was, according to its authors, an attempt to capture only the important features of the complicated and sophisticated ALGOL. However, like ALGOL, CPL was large with many features that were hard to learn. In an attempt at further simplification, Martin Richards of Cambridge developed a subset of CPL called BCPL (Basic Computer Programming Language, 1967). In 1970 Ken Thompson of Bell Labs developed yet another simplification of CPL called simply B, in connection with an early implementation of the UNIX operating system.

The development of integrated circuits (IC) signaled the beginning of the third generation. ICs were single, complete electronic semiconductor circuits contained on a piece of silicon, sometimes called chips. Memory also improved. By 1969, 1, 000 transistors could be built on a chip of silicon. Magnetic disks could save more, and monitors and keyboards   102 troduced to replace punched cards. A new program, the operating system, was also introduced, meaning that human operators were no longer needed. High-level programming languages continued to be developed, including RPG and Pascal .

A new concept in this generation was that of a family of computers, which allowed computers to be upgraded and expanded as necessary. This was addressed originally by IBM with its IBM/360 series which had programs which were also compatible with any other machine in the line.

Examples : NCR 395, B6500, IBM 360,370

<u>Characteristics of third generation computers</u>

- These computers were based on integrated circuit(IC) technology.
- Computational time reduced from microseconds to nanoseconds.
- More portable, more reliable than second generation computers.
- Consumed less power and generate less heat.
- Size of these computers smaller than as compared to pervious computers.
- Maintenance cost less, since failing hardware occurred very rarely.
- High-level languages were used to program computer.

8.1.4 Fourth Generations (1972-1984) : Microprocessors

The next generation of computer systems saw the use of large scale integration (LSI - 1000 devices per chip) and very large scale integration (VLSI - 100,000 devices per chip) in the construction of computing elements. At this scale entire processors will fit onto a single chip, and for simple systems the entire computer (processor, main memory, and I/O controllers) can fit on one chip. Gate delays dropped to about 1ns per gate.

Semiconductor memories replaced core memories as the main memory in most systems; until this time the use of semiconductor memory in most systems was limited to registers and cache. During th ^{103} d, high speed vector processors, such as the CRAY 1, CRAY X-MP and CYBER 205 dominated the high performance computing scene. Computers with large main memory, such as the CRAY 2, began to emerge. A variety of parallel architectures began to appear; however, during this period the parallel computing efforts were of a mostly experimental nature and most computational science was carried out on vector processors. Microcomputers and workstations were introduced and saw wide use as alternatives to time-shared mainframe computers.

Developments in software include very high level languages such as FP (functional programming) and Prolog (programming in logic). These languages tend to use a declarative programming style as opposed to the imperative style of Pascal, C, FORTRAN, et al. In a declarative style, a programmer gives a mathematical specification of what should be computed, leaving many details of how it should be computed to the compiler and/or runtime system. These languages are not yet in wide use, but are very promising as notations for programs that will run on massively parallel computers (systems with over 1,000 processors). Compilers for established languages started to use sophisticated optimization techniques to improve code, and compilers for vector processors were able to vectorize simple loops (turn loops into single instructions that would initiate an operation over an entire vector.

Two important events marked the early part of the third generation: the development of the C programming language and the UNIX operating system, both at Bell Labs. In 1972, Dennis Ritchie, seeking to meet the design goals of CPL and generalize Thompson's B, developed the C language. Thompson and Ritchie then used C to write a version of UNIX for the DEC PDP-11. This C- based UNIX was soon ported to many different computers, relieving users from having to learn a new operating system each time they change computer
hardware. UNIX or a derivative of UNIX is now a de facto standard on virtually every computer system.

An important event in the development of computational science was thepublication of the Lax report. In 1982, the US Department of Defense (DOD) and National Science Foundation (NSF) sponsored a panel on Large Scale Computing in Science and Engineering, chaired by Peter D. Lax. The Lax Report stated that aggressive and focused foreign initiatives in high performance computing, especially in Japan, were in sharp contrast to the absence of coordinat ed national attention in the United States. The report noted that university researchers had inadequate access to high performance computers. One of the first and most visible of the responses to the Lax report was the establishment of the NSF supercomputing centers. Phase I on this NSF program was designed to encourage the use of high performance computing at American universities by making cycles and training on three (and later six) existing supercomputers immediately available. Following this Phase I stage, in 1984-1985 NSF provided funding for the establishment of five Phase II supercomputing centers.

The Phase II centers, located in San Diego (San Diego Supercomputing Center); Illinois (National Center for Supercomputing Applications); Pittsburgh (Pittsburgh Supercomputing Center); Cornell (Cornell Theory Center); and Princeton (John von Neumann Center), have been extremely successful at providing computing time on supercomputers to the academic community. In addition they have provided many valuable training programs and have developed several software packages that are available free of charge. These Phase II centers continue to augment the substantial high performance computing efforts at the National Laboratories, especially the Department of Energy (DOE) and NASA sites.

After the integrated circuit, the only place to go was down - in size, that is. Large scale integration (LSI) could fit hundreds of components onto one chip. By the

1980's, very large scale integration (VLSI) squeezed hundreds of thousands of

components onto a chip. The ability to fit so much onto an area about half the size of a U.S. dime helped diminish the size and price of computers. It also increased their power, efficiency and reliability. Marcian Hoff invented a device which could replace several of the components of earlier computers, the microprocessor. The microprocessor is the characteristic of fourth generation computers, capable of performing all of the functions of a computer's central processing unit. The reduced size, reduced cost, and increased speed of the microprocessor led to the creation of the first personal computers. Until now computers had been the almost exclusively the domain of universities, business and government. In 1976, Steve Jobs and Steve Wozniak built the Apple II, the first personal computer in a garage in California. Then, in 1981, IBM introduced its first personal computer. The personal computer was such a revolutionary concept and was expected to have such an impact on society that in 1982, "Time" magazine dedicated its annual "Man of the Year Issue" to the computer. The other feature of the microprocessor is its versatility. Whereas previously the integrated circuit had had to be manufactured to fit a special purpose, now one microprocessor could be manufactured and then programmed to meet any number of demands. Soon everyday household items such as microwave ovens, television sets and automobiles with electronic fuel injection incorporated microprocessors. The 1980's saw an expansion in computer use in all three arenas as clones of the IBM PC made the personal computer even more affordable. The number of personal computers in use more than doubled from 2 million in 1981 to 5.5 million in 1982. Ten years later, 65 million PCs were being used. Computers continued their trend toward a smaller size, working their way down from desktop to laptop computers (which could fit inside a briefcase) to palmtop (able to fit inside a breast pocket).

Examples : Apple II, Alter 8800, CRAY-1

Characteristics of fourth generation computers

- These computers are microprocessor-based systems.

- These computers are very small in size.

- These are cheapest among all other generations discussed above.

- They are portable and reliable.

- Minimum maintenance cost required since hardware failure is negligible.

- Interconnection of computers leads to better communication and resource sharing.

8.1.5 Fifth Generation (1984-) : Artificial Language

The development of the next generation of computer systems is characterized mainly by the acceptance of parallel processing. Until this time parallelism was limited to pipelining and vector processing, or at most to a few processors sharing jobs. The fifth generation saw the introduction of machines with hundreds of processors that could all be working on different parts of a single program. The scale of integration in semiconductors continued at an incredible pace - by 1990 it was possible to build chips with a million components - and semiconductor memories became standard on all computers.

Other new developments were the widespread use of computer networks and the
increasing use of single-user workstations. Prior to 1985 large scale parallel processing was viewed as a research goal, but two systems introduced around this time are typical of the first commercial products to be based on parallel processing. The Sequent Balance 8000 connected up to 20 processors to a single shared memory module (but each processor had its own local cache). The machine was designed to compete with the DEC VAX-780 as a general purpose Unix system, with each processor working on a different user's job. However Sequent provided a library of subroutines that would allow programmers to write programs that would use more than one processor, and the machine was widely used to explore parallel algorithms and programming techniques.

The Intel iPSC-1, nicknamed ``the hypercube", took a different approach. Instead
of using one memory module, Intel connected each processor to its own memory and used a network interface to connect processors. This distributed memory architecture meant memory was no longer a bottleneck and large systems (using more processors) could be built. The largest iPSC-1 had 128 processors. Toward
the end of this period a third type of parallel processor was introduced to the market. In this style of machine, known as a data-parallel or SIMD, there are several thousand very simple processors. All processors work under the direction
of a single control unit; i.e. if the control unit says ``add a to b" then all processors find their local copy of a and add it to their local copy of b.

Machines in this class

include the Connection Machine from Thinking Machines, Inc., and the MP-1 from MasPar, Inc.

Scientific computing in this period was still dominated by vector processing. Most

manufacturers of vector processors introduced parallel models, but there were very few (two to eight) processors in this parallel machines. In the area of computer networking, both wide area network (WAN) and local area network (LAN) technology developed at a rapid pace, stimulating a transition from the traditional mainframe computing environment toward a distributed computing environment in which each user has their own workstation for relatively simple tasks (editing and compiling programs, reading mail) but sharing large, expensive resources such as file servers and supercomputers. RISC technology (a style of internal organization of the CPU) and plummeting costs for RAM brought tremendous gains in computational power of relatively low cost workstations and servers. This period also saw a marked increase in both the quality and quantity of scientific visualization.

Anticipated new type of computer based on emerging microelectronic technologies with high computing speeds and parallel processing. The development of very large-scale integration (VLSI) technology, which can put many more circuits onto an integrated circuit (chip) than is currently possible, and developments in computer hardware and software design may produce computers far more powerful than those in current use.

It has been predicted that such a computer will be able to communicate in natural spoken language with its user; store vast knowledge databases; search rapidly through these databases, making intelligent inferences and drawing logical conclusions; and process images and 'see' objects in the way that humans do.

Characteristics of fifth generation computers

• These computers are super very scale integrated chips(SVSIC)- based systems.

• These computers use intelligent programming and knowledge based problem solving techniques.

• These computers have input and output in the form images or speeches.

• These computers required a great amount of storage capacity.

• These computers have parallel processing capability.

****

CHAPTER – 9
Computers and Communications

STRUCTURE:

9.0 Objective

9.1 Introduction

9.2 Types of communications with and among computers.

9. 3 Need for computer communication networks.

9.0 OBJECTIVES:

We live in the computer oriented society and we are constantly bombarded with a multitude of terms relating to the computers. With the conclusion of this chapter we should be able to explain the computer related terms, communication networks , internet fundam e ntals and flow of inform ation through different form s of channel.

9.1   INTRODUCTION:

Early computers were being used as "stand-alone" systems in organizations fulfilling their own requirements. With widespread use of computers there was a realization that it would be advantageous in many situations to use computers from remote points. It was also felt that connecting computers together via telecommunication lines will lead to widespread availability of powerful computers. Advances in computers technology also made these interconnections possible. In that chapter we will discuss various aspects of communications technology and examine how this technology can be used along with computer technology to provide powerful networks of computers.

9.2   TYPES   OF   COMMUNICATIONS   WITH   AND   AMONG COMPUTERS

We are aware about the need and advantages of time sharing of a computer among many users by using interactive terminals. Users would prefer to have access to a computer from their place of work or even their homes without having to go to the computer centre. Such access can be provided by connecting the users' terminals by communication lines to the computer. As a user, working at a terminal, enters program and data manually, the speed of communication to the computer is slow. The method does not place heavy demands on the communication lines.

Another type of communication between computers would be necessary when a number of computers close together (within 10 km radius) are to be connected together. An organization may have a number of computers in different locations in a campus, each computer fulfilling a function. For instance, an office may have a computer which is used as a word processor and a filing system, the stores department may have a small computer for inventory control, the accounts department may have a computer to compute payroll, prepare budgets, etc. An interconnection of these machines would be useful to share files, to transfer the load from one of the machines to the other when a machine breaks down and to exchange messages between departments. Such a connection of computers is called a Local Area Network, LAN for short. In this case fast communication is required between machines. Besides this, the traffic between computers will be in short bursts of intense activity.

Suppose an organization has a powerful computer with large disks for file storage, fast printers etc. It may have many branch offices in many cities with their own smaller computers, small disk, printer etc. For many applications in the branch office it may find its local computer and data base sufficient. There may be instances when branch offices need a more powerful computer. In such a case it would be necessary to use the computer in the main office from terminals in the branch offices and transfer the result files back to the branch office for printing locally. Very often information such as local sales reports, accounts etc., may have to be transferred to the main office by the branch offices to update the organizational data base. Such a connection of a number of computers in known as Computer Network. In this case it would be necessary to use communication media maintained by post and telegraph or telephone companies. Such communication networks are known as public networks or common carrier networks. These networks usually have land telephone lines, underground coaxial cables, microwave communication and satellite communications. These networks are normally designed for human telephone conversation or low speed telegraph transmission and need to be adapted for computer to computer communication.

In view of the increasing requirement for high speed data communications, the public networks in various countries of the world are being improved. Data communications lines which transmit data at 64K bits/second are now easily available. New systems are being introduced which will communicate data at the rate of 2M bits/second over long distances.

Another type of communication which is becoming very important is transmission of data between computer networks. This is called internetworking. Various networks within a country can be interconnected. Country networks can in turn be connected to networks in other countries. In this case one needs interoperability. By interoperability we mean the ability of diverse computers from different vendors and with different operating systems to cooperate in solving computational problems. It should be possible for users to use the network without knowing the details of the hardware, communication method etc. Such a worldwide network is now available and is called the Internet. Internet is now widely used all over the world including India.

9.3   NEED FOR COMPUTER COMMUNICATION NETWORKS

Here is the detailed description regarding the computer communication discussed in the last section. Remote time sharing terminals are most useful for program development. The rapid turn around provided by such a use increases programmer productivity. A user who has a personal computer at home would use it for most of his work and connect the video terminal of the personal computer to a big computer for solving larger programs and to access special library programs and date resident in the big computers.

Another use is by smaller organizations which may not have the work load to justify an in-house computers. In such a case they buy a workstation or a PC, place it in their premises and connect it as a time-sharing terminal to a larger computer via a telephone line. This allows them to conveniently access a larger machine without having to make frequent trips to the computer centre.

Another important remote terminal application is for information retrieval. Some information centres store large amounts of data on patents, technical report, journal articles, etc., in an organized fashion. A user requiring specific information, say on patents in a specified area, can connect his terminal through a telephone line to a large computer and retrieve the

115

information using appropriate descriptors. Some information centres are connected to the international fax networks and it would be possible to send enquiries via fax to such centres. Rapidly many such centres are being connected to internet. Enquiries and replies would then be by electronic mail.

As we saw in the last section, local area networks are used to interconnect many computers within an organization. The purpose of interconnection would be to share files, share programs, and decentralize specialized functions. Another reason for creating a local network is also to share the use of expensive peripherals such as fast printers, large disks, graphics workstations, etc. Similar local networks are useful in a laboratory environment where each sophisticated instrument has a built-in microprocessor. These can be interconnected and the network connected in turn to a general purpose computer with powerful I/O devices and storage devices. The general purpose computer and the peripheral devices enhance the power for analyzing the output of each of the instruments. Besides this, data gathered and processed by each instrument may be correlated.

Local area networks are also used in factories for controlling plants and processes. Individual small computers would be usually installed to monitor and control critical processes in the plant. These computers may be interconnected and connected in turn to another computer which would perform supervisory functions. Such a network provides an integrated control of the plant.

The communication lines interconnecting the computers in LAN are short. It is also localized to "private" area and one need not use a public telephone network. As distances are small and as faster communication between processors in the LAN is desirable, high speed communication lines which can transmit around ten million to hundred million bits per second are used to interconnect them.

CHAPTER – 10
Computers Networks

STRUCTURE:

10.0 OBJECTIVES:

A network is a series of interconnections that form a cohesive and ubiquitous connectivity arrangem e nts when tied together. Whew! That sounds ominous but, but to make this a little simpler, let's look at the com ponents of what constitutes the com m unication network. Different network topologies will be covered in the chapter.

10.1   COMPUTER NETWORK TOPLOGIES

When computers at different locations are to be interconnected one may do it in a number of ways. For example, if five computers A, B, C, D, E are to be interconnected we may do it as shown in Fig. 8.1. In this case there are physical links between A-C, A-E, D-C, B-E and B-D. Assuming full duplex links, A can communicate with C and E, B with E and D, C with A and D, D with B and C, and E with A and B. Direct communication between A and B and A and D is not possible. If, however, C can route a message from A to D then there would be a logical connection between A and D. Similarly E can communicate with D via B and C with B via D. Each computer in the network will be called a node.

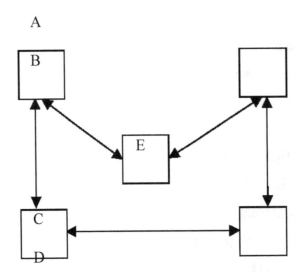

Fig10.1 A ring connection of computers

The main considerations in selecting a particular topology are:

(i)   The availability and cost of physical communication lines between nodes and line bandwidth.

(ii)   The capability of a node to route information to other nodes.

(iii)   Delays due to routing of information.

(iv)   Reliability of communication between nodes when there is a breakdown of a line on a node.

(v)   Strategy of controlling communication between nodes in the network-centralized or distributed.

The fully connected topology of has a separate physical connection for connecting each node to any other node. It is the most expensive system from the point of view of the line costs, as there are 10 separate point-to-point lines. It is, however, very reliable as any line breakdown will affect only communication between the connected machines. Each node need not have individual routing capability. Communication is very fast between any two nodes. The control is distributed, with each computer deciding its communication priorities.

The star topology has minimum line cost as only 4 lines are used. The routing function is performed by E which centrally controls communication between any two nodes by establishing a logical path between them. Thus if A wants to communicate with D, E would received this request from A and set up and logical path A-E-D based on line availability. Delays would not increase when new nodes are added as any two nodes may be connected via two links only. The system, however, crucially depends on E. If E breaks down the whole network would break down.

The ring topology of is not centrally controlled. Each node must have simple communication capability. A node will receive date from one of its two neighbors. The only decision the node has to take is whether the data is for its use or not. If the data is not addressed to it, it merely passes it on to its other neighbor. Thus if E receives data from B it examines whether it is addressed to self. If it is, then it uses the data, else it passes the data to A.

The main disadvantage of a ring is larger communication delays if the number of nodes increase. It is, however, more reliable than a star network because communication is not dependent on a single computer. If one line between any two computers breaks down, of ir any of the computers breaks down, alternate routing is possible.

One may use a hybrid approach to interconnection. In other words, theinterconnection may not be a pure star, loop or full interconnection. The physical links may be set up based on the criteria specified at the beginning of the section to have an optimal communication capability for the specified network functions.

Another interconnection method is a multipoint or multi drop linkage of computers shown in Fig.8.4. The main advantage of this method is the reduction in physical lines. One line is shared by all nodes. If computer A wants to communicate with E then it first checks whether the communication line is free. When the line becomes free it transmits the message addressed to E on it. As the message travels on the line, each computers checks whether it is addressed to it. In this case when E finds its "address" in the message it accepts it, sends an acknowledgement to A and frees the line. Thus each computers connected to the line must have good communication and decision making capability.

An alternate approach which can free each machine of this task is to have one master computer overseeing communications on the line. The master would receive all messages and route them to appropriate machine. This approach would however create a bottleneck when computers connected to the link increase and consequently the master computer becomes too busy.

The method whereby each computer in a multi drop configuration places a message with the source and destinations addresses, to be picked up by the addresses, is known as a broadcast scheme. This method is appropriate for use in a local area network where a high speed communication channel is used and computers are confined to a small area. This method is also appropriate when satellite communication is used as one satellite channel may be shared by many computers at a number of geographical locations. In this method it is easy to add new computers to the network. The reliability of the network will be high with distributed control because the failure of a computer in the network functioning for other computers.

10.4 COMMUNICATION PROTOCOLS

When a number of computers and terminal equipment are to be connected together to form an integrated system, a well understood standard method of communication and physical interconnection should be established. This becomes particularly critical when equipment supplied by different vendors are to be connected since every vendor would have his own standards. If computers in different countries are to be connected together, yet another

120

problem arises due to the need to use communication systems belonging to different nations which would have their own telecommunication regulations. Common agreed rules followed to interconnect and communicate between computers are known as protocols.

A universally used standard method of interconnecting user terminalsto computers is the one proposed by Electronic Industries Association (USA) standard RS 232-C. This standard has been endorsed by CCITT (Commite' Counsultatif International Telegraphique or Telephonique) recommendation V24. It completely specifies the interface between data communication devices (for example, modems), computers, and terminals. The RS 232-C interface consists of 25 connection points which specify the physical pin connections, voltage levels, signals transmission rates, timing information and control information such as ready and send.

The interconnection protocol for computer to computer communication is much more complex. It should define, besides the physical characteristics such as voltage levels, speeds, etc.., the following:

(I)   How to begin and terminate a session between two computers?

(II)   How the messages in a session are to be framed?

(III)   How errors in transmission of messages are to be detected?

(IV)   How messages are to be retransmitted when errors are detected?

(V)   How to find out which message block was sent by which terminal/computers and to whom?

(vi)   How the dialogue on the communication line proceeds?

The most common method of sharing communication lines in a network is for a central communication controller to allocate unique addresses to computers and terminals in the network and allocate resources by polling. In polling, the communications controller asks a terminal or computer, using its address, whether a message block is to be sent. If the answer is 'yes' it accepts the message and routes it to the computer or terminal specified, if it free to receive it.

Although no manufacturer supports another's data communications protocols, several protocols are available. One popular protocol is International Business Machines (IBM) System Data Link Control (SDLC).

The other telecommunication protocols are National Cash Register's (NCR) BISYNC, Burrough's Data Link Control, Honeywell Data Link Control and DECNET.

An interconnection protocol for computer to computer communication as recommended by International Standards Organization (ISO) is gaining wide acceptance. It is an approach based on defining a number of distinct layers each addressing itself to one aspect of linking. This is known as the ISO model for open systems interconnection. The ISO model is made up of seven layers as shown in Fig. 8.5. Each layer has a specific independent function. The standardization achieved by each of the layers is explained in what follows:

Physical link layer: This layer defines the electrical and mechanical aspects of interfacing to a physical medium for transmitting data. It also defines how physical links are set up, maintained and disconnected.

Data Link layer : This layer establishes an error-free communications path between computers over the physical channel. It gives the standard for framing messages, checking integrity of received messages, accessing and using channels and sequencing of transmitted data.

Network control layer: This determines the setting up of a logical path between computers in a network, message addressing to computers, andcontrolling message flow between computer nodes.

Transport layer: Once a path is established between computers it provides control standards for a communication session for enabling processes to exchange data reliably and sequentially, independent of which systems are communicating or their location in the network.

Session control layer: This establishes and controls system dependent aspects of communications session between specific computers in the network and bridges the gap between the services provided by the transport layer and the logical functions running under the operating system of a particular computers in the network.

Presentation control layer: This layer provides facilities to convert encoded transmitted data into forms which can be displayed on a video terminal or printed.

Application/user layer: This provides services that directly support users such as file transfers, remote file access, data base management etc.

The main advantage of the layered approach is that each one can be improved and modified independent of other layers. With changes in communication technology and standards, easy adaptation is important. One standard which defines the first three layers of ISO is the CCITT X.25 protocol. This standard has been integrated in the network architecture of many vendors.

In an ideal computer network, a user working at any one of the computers at any location in the network should be able to utilize the special facilities, languages, etc., available in any other computers in the network without having to know the detailed filing methods, the type of operating system commands, etc. of that machine. In other words, there should be a standard user interface at all locations. The network operating system should be able to decide and provide the optimal computing facility to a user to fulfil his requirements wherever he may be in the network without his having to even know from where and how his requirements are met.

10.3   LOCAL AREA NETWORKS

When computers located within a small geographical area such as an office or a University Camput (Within a radius of 10 kms) are connected together we call it a Local Area Network (LAN). The topology of connection of computers in a LAN are:

(i) A star network.

(ii) A multidrop (or a bus based) network.

(iii) A ring .

Among these the star network usually uses a local telephone exchange to connect computers. In other words the node E (in Fig. 8.2) is a telephone exchange. This is not a very popular arrangement as an exchange failure leads to LAN failure. Data transmission rates via an exchange is also restricted. Among the other two LAN topologies, the multidrop or bus topology is very popular as it is not expensive, standardized and supported by all computer vendors. It is called an Ethernet connection. (Ether was originally thought of the medium through which electromagnetic waves are propagated). Ethernet allows data transmission at the rate of 10 Mbps (10 million bits per second).

The ring topology is now being used for highly reliable high speed LANs using fibre optic transmission medium. A standard has emerged known as Fibre Distributed Data Interface (FDDI) for ring networks using Fibre Optic cables. It is now supported by all vendors of workstations. This standard allows transmission speed of 100 Mpbs.

In the rest of this section we will discuss in detail the characteristics of Ethernet LAN and FDDI LAN.

There are two types of Local Area Network:

1   Ethernet Local Area Network
2   FDDI Local Area Network

10.3.1 Ethernet Local Area Network

Ethernet is a standard developed by Digital Equipment Corporation, Xerox and Intel for interconnecting computers within a small geographic area. This was later refined and standardized as IEEE standards 802. The standard specifies interconnection of computers using a bus. The physical layer is a shielded co-axial cable supporting a data rate of 10 Mbps. The maximum length of the cable is 2.8 km and the maximum number of nodes which can be connected is 1024.

The data link layer defines controlling access to the network and how data packets are transmitted between stations connected to the network station communicates with the bus via a transceiver, that is, a combined transmitter and receiver.

Each station sends packets as a set of coded bits which are not modulated. Modulation is not necessary as the maximum length of the cable is small. Transmission of bits on the cable with out modulation is known as base band transmission. Exchange of data between stations proceeds as per the following protocols. When a station wants to send data, its receiver listens to the bus to find out whether any signal is being transmitted on the bus. This is called Carrier Server (CS). If no signal is detected it transmits a data packets. As the bus is accessible to all stations connected to it more than one station could find no signal on the bus and try to transmit a packet on the bus. If more than one station transmits a packet on the bus than these packets will collide and both packets will be spoiled. Thus the receiver part of the transceiver of the station must listen to the bus for a minimum period T to see if any collision occurred. The period T is that time which the packet will take to reach the farthest station in the bus and return back to the sender. Collision is detected if the energy level of signal in the bus suddenly increases. Once a collision is detected the station which detected the collision sends a jamming signal which is sensed by all other stations on the bus so that they do not try to transmit any packet. The station also stops transmitting and waits for a random time and retransmits the packet. As it waited for a random time the probability of another collision is low. If there is again a collision it waits for double the previous random period and transmits. By experiments and analysis it is found that this method is quit effective and collision less transmission will take place soon. This method of accessing the bus and transmitting packet is known as Carrier Sense Multiple Access with Collision Detection (CSMA/CD) System. It is called multiple accesses as any of the stations can try to send a packet on the bus or receive a packet from the bus.

The format of a packet consists of some bits for clock synchronization followed by the address of the sender, address of the receiver, data packet and check bits. A packet sent by a station is monitored while it is in transit by all other station on the bus and the station to which it is addressed receives the packet and stores it. Other stations ignore it. It is possible to broadcast a packet to all stations. A packet can also be multicast that is, sent to a sub-set of stations.

The length of the packet is between 64 and 1518 bytes. The length is based on the length of the bus and number of stations connected to the bus. Currently Ethernet is one of most popular LANs used as it is well proven, standardized and supported by all venders of computers. Cheaper versions of Ethernet are now emerging. One of them is the use of unshielded twisted pair of wires in stead of a co-axial cable. This has become possible due to improvement in electronics technology. The speed of these LANs is also 10 Mbps.

Another system using Ethernet protocol is called thin wire Ethernet. This uses a standard co-axial cable like those used in cable TV. TV cables are mass manufactured and are cheaper. Workstation manufactures have designed a simple digital electronic circuit known as Ethernet Interface Card. This can connect to the thin wire net thereby reducing cost further. Thin Ethernet wire supports fewer workstations over a shorter distance compared to the Ethernet standards.

Ethernets may be extended using a hardware unit called a repeater. A repeater reshapes and amplifies the signal and relays it from one Ethernet segment to another. A typical use of repeaters is shown in figure 8.8 in an office. A backbone cable runs vertically up the building. A repeater is used to attach Ethernet segments running in each floor to the backbone. Each Ethernet segment is usually limited to 500 meters. No two workstations can

have more than two repeaters between then if they have to communicate reliably. Use of repeaters is an inexpensive way of interconnecting Ethernets. The main disadvantage of repeaters is they repeat any noise in the system and are prone to failure as they require separate power supply and are active elements unlike a cable which is passive.

Recently wireless LANs are also appearing in the market. They use wireless transceiver and packet radio transmission between stations.

10.3.2 FDDI Local Area Network

Fiber Distributed Data Interface (FDDI) is a standard defined by ISO/ANSI and IEEE for LANs using fiber optic cables to interconnect workstations/computers in the network. The standard defines the two lower most layers of the ISO protocol. The physical layer medium dependent standard defines the specification of optical transmitters and receivers, fiber optic cable, media interface connectors and optical bypass relays (optional). The transmitter is a LED and the receiver is a photo detector. LED are inexpensive. The fiber optic cable defined in the original standard 62.5 micrometer core diameter multimode, graded index, fiber optic cable with a cladding diameter of 125 micrometer(known as 62.5/125 cable). The connector mechanical details are given to connect to workstation ports. A relay is send to bypass the workstation/computer when the work station fails. The media standards are being modified to include both copper cables and single mode optical fiber. The other part of the physical layer standard specifies the methods of encoding data and synchronizing signals between workstations.

The next layer, namely, the data link layer, defines how the workstations are connected and how they access the network and communicate with one another FDDI network consists of dual counter rotating rings. The stations are connected by a primary ring and a secondary or backup ring (Fig 8.9(a)). The primary ring carries the data between stations where as the secondary ring aids in initializing the ring, reconfiguring and provides backup to ten primary ring. Each ring in FDDI standard cannot exceed 100km. The dual ring allows the transmission if one of the station fails or a cable breaks. This is done by wrapping around using the secondary ring. Thus the FDDI standard provides excellent fault tolerance. If both faults occur than FDDI can be broken up into multiple independent ring. The FDDI ring is designed to transmit data at 100 Mbps.

Frames are transmitted between stations in a FDDI ring using a protocol called the Timed Token Protocol (TTP). A token is a unique symbol sequence which circulates around the ring. To transmit a data station A does the following:

1.   It waits for a free token to arrive and captures it.

2.   It sets up a frame to be sent, appends a token to it and puts it out on the ring. The frame consists of some preamble bits followed by addresses of the destination station and the source station, the data packet to be sent and check bits.

3.   It waits for a free token to arrive and captures it.

4.   It sets up a frame to be sent, appends a token to it and puts it out on the ring. The frame consists of some preamble bits followed by addresses of the destination station and the source station, the data packet to be sent and check bits.

5.   When station B in the ring receives the frame it checks it is intended for it by matching the destination address with its own address. If it is meant for it, it copies the packet and puts it back on the ring. It also checks for errors, if any, and notes it in the frame. If the frame is not addressed to it, it just forwards the frame to the next station C.

6.   After receiving the frame the station B would receive the token sent by

the first station. If it wants to transmit a frame it can do it as explained in 2. Else it puts the token back in the ring.

7.   The frame sent by A is read by C and forwarded to D after checking and noting errors if any.

8.   D in turn receives the packet and forwards it to A.

9.   When A gets the frame it knows from the source address that it was the originator of the frame. If no error indication is in the frame it deletes the frame. If there is an error indication it retransmits the frame when it receives the token.

10.   If station A does not receive the frame with in a specified time there is a possibility of failure in the ring. It then sends a special frame called a BEACON. And checks if it returns to it within a specified time. If not , a break is signaled

Observe that after a sent frame and releases the token, B can capture it and send a frame and a token which C can capture and send a frame and finally D can send a frame.

The FDDI standard allows all stations synchronous data transfer for a specified period followed by asynchronous transmission the time allowed for each of this is dependent upon the time taken by a token to complete one rotation of the ring. The protocol allows a fair allocation of time to all the stations in the ring to transmit data.

10.4 INTERCONNECTING NETWORKS

We examined Local Area Networks in the last section. LANs connect machines in a small geographical area (around 1 km radius) and can operate 4 Mbps to 2 Gbps (Gigabits per second). Networks which connect machines in larger geographic areas are known as Metropolitan Area Networks (MANs) and Wide Area Networks (WANs). MANs operate over an area of around 100 km radius at a speed between 56 Kbps and 100 Mbps. Wide Area Networks, are known as long haul networks, operate over the entire world with speeds in the range of 9.6 Kbps to 45 Mbps.

To build a large network, smaller networks are interconnected. We already saw in the last section how small Ethernet segments in a building can be connected together using repeaters to create a larger LAN. Repeater is the lowest level interconnect device which connects physical layers. It amplifies and reshapes electrical signals (bits) and retransmits them. The next level interconnect device is called a bridge. A bridge is designed to store and forward frames one LAN to another. They are ideally invisible to the end stations which communicate and are located in different LANs. Routers steer traffic through multiple LANs and ensure that the least congested route istaken. Traffic within a LAN are not disturbed by a router. Unlike bridges routers are known to the end stations so that they can send messages to them to find out about frames sent by them.

When larger networks are built interconnecting smaller networks one should have as the main goal interoperability. By interoperability we mean the ability of software and hardware of multiple machines from multiple vendors to communicate and operate together meaningfully. This is achieved to a great extend by a world wide computer network known as Internet. This network is a collection of interconnected packet switched networks using a protocol called Transmission Control Protocol abbreviated as TCP/IP. This protocol does not follow the ISO/OSI protocol. It may be thought of as dealing with the higher layers, namely, the transport and application layers of ISO/OSI mode. TCP/IP defines the unit of data transmission as a datagram and specifies how to transmit data grams on a particular network.

10.5 COMMUNICATION PROTOCOLS

Internet allows any pair of computers attached to it to communicate. Each computer is assigned an address which is universally recognized throughout the network. Every datagram carries the address of its source and destination. Intermediate switching computers (routers) use destination address to route datagrams. TCP/IP provides acknowledgements between source and destination. The other transport level service provided by TCP/IP besides packet delivery is a reliable stream transport service. In other words, it "connects" an application program on one computer with the another one, and allows sending of large volumes of data between them as though they were connected directly by hardware. In order to achieve this, the protocol makes the sender divide the stream of data into small messages (data grams) and send them, one at a time, waiting for the receiver to acknowledge receipt. In addition to providing basic transport-level services the TCP/IP. For all practical purposes TCP/IP has become the standard for internetworking in Wide Area Networks (WANs).

While talking more technical TCP/IP is a collection of protocols. The base protocol described by the letters TCP/IP refer to the lower three or four layers of the OSI model. Some layer 7 protocols ride on the top of TCP/IP. Among these are FTP, Telnet, simple mail transfer protocol (SMTP)and simple network management protocol (SNMP). Newer protocols like the real time protocols (RTP) and the network time sharp (NTP) ride at layer 7.

FTP stands for the file transfer protocol. When you use a browser to ,access a list of files or updates to programs on a website, when you actually click on an icon or the link to receive a file, there's a better-than-even chance that the file is being retrieved using FTP. FTP is not the protocol used for the routine browser operations, but the major browsers do incorporate the capability of moving files around using FTP. FTP existed long before the world wide web.

Telnet is a means to sign onto a remote system network directly as a user. This is not the same as using the world wide web, although the physical infrastructure is the same. When you use a browser to access a web page, every time you click on a link, you send a request for a specific set of information to a specific website. That website, if it can, sends back just the information you have requested. Telnet enables signing on to the remote computer.

You cannot use SMTP protocol explicitly; however, if you use internet mail, then you are using SMTP protocol. As mail protocol go . SMTP is pretty simple to use. Although among the least sophisticated mail environments in the world, SMTP mail is sort of taking over the world. Why? Because SMTP is built into pretty much all systems that use the internet. It is the kind of mail that you get when you sign up with ISP.

SMNP protocol is integral to the management of the internet, most usres will never be involved with the SNMP because it is used by the people operating the Internet rather than by its end users.

10.5 ASYNCHRONOUS TRANSFER MODE (ATM)

Asynchronous transfer mode (ATM) is one of a class of the packet switching technologies that relays traffic via an address contained with in the packet. Packet-switching techniques are not new; some have been around since the late 1960s. However, when packet switching was first developed, the packets used variable length of information. This variable length of the each packet caused some latency within the network because the processing equipment used special timers and delimiters to ensure that all the data was enclosed in the packet. As a next step toward creating a faster packet switching service, the industry introduced the concept of frame relay. Both of the packet switching concepts (X.25 a layer 3 and the other [frame relay] a layer 2 protocol) used variable length packets. To overcome this overhead and latency, a fixed cell size was introduced. In early 1992, the industry adopted a fast packet, or cell relay, concept that uses a short 53 byte , fixed length cell to transmit information across both private and public networks. This cell relay technique was introduced as ATM.ATM represents a specific type of cell relay that is introduce as defined in the general category of the overall broad band ISDN (B-ISDN) standard. In fact when we are talking about B-ISDN we are talking about ATM.

ATM is defined as a transport and switching method in which information does not occur periodically with some reference, such as a frame pattern. All other techniques used a fixed timing reference; **ATM does not:** hence the name asynchronous. With ATM, the data arrives and is processed across the network randomly. No specific timing is associated with the ATM traffic, so the cells are generated as the data needs to be transmitted. When no traffic exists, idle cells may be present on the network, or cells carrying over payloads will be present.

What ATM basically is?

ATM is a telecommunications concept defined by American National Standards Institute (ANSI) and International Telecommunications Union (ITU) standards committees for the transport of a broad range of user information including voice, data and video communications on any user-to-

131

network interface (UNI). Because the ATM concept covers these services, it might as well be positioned as the high speed networking tool of the 1990's and beyond. ATM can be used to aggregate user traffic from multiple existing applications onto a single UNI. The current version of UNI is 4.0 which specifies the rate of speed and the agreed-to throughput at the user interface. ATM concept aggregates a myriad of services onto a single access arrangement

All the sec services can be combined at the aggregate rates of upto 622 Mbps today for the user traffic. However; the end user future rates of speed will be in the 1.2 to 2.4 Gbps class. Currently, the carriers are using the speed of 622 Mbps across their backbone networks, but will be deploying the 2.4 Gbps soon. In future, the carriers will step upto 10 Gbps and higher rates.

One can now see why the networking and the service internetworking functions are so important. Millions of dollars of investment can still be used, and newer protocols can be deployed without making the entire network obsolete. This is what internetworking is all about.

***

www.ingramcontent.com/pod-product-compliance
Lightning Source LLC
Chambersburg PA
CBHW080426060326
40689CB00019B/4399